THIS IS geography

JOHN WIDDOWSON

3

HODDER EDUCATION
AN HACHETTE UK COMPANY

Although every effort has been made to ensure that website addresses are correct at time of going to press, Hodder Education cannot be held responsible for the content of any website mentioned in this book. It is sometimes possible to find a relocated web page by typing in the address of the home page for a website in the URL window of your browser.

Hachette Livre UK's policy is to use papers that are natural, renewable and recyclable products and made from wood grown in sustainable forests. The logging and manufacturing processes are expected to conform to the environmental regulations of the country of origin.

Orders: please contact Bookpoint Ltd, 130 Milton Park, Abingdon, Oxon OX14 4SB. Telephone: +44 (0)1235 827720. Fax: +44 (0)1235 400454. Lines are open 9.00–5.00, Monday to Saturday, with a 24-hour message answering service. Visit our website at www.hoddereducation.co.uk

© John Widdowson 2009
First published in 2009 by Hodder Education,
A Hachette UK company
338 Euston Road
London NW1 3BH

Impression number   5 4 3 2 1
Year   2013 2012 2011 2010 2009

All rights reserved. Apart from any use permitted under UK copyright law, no part of this publication may be reproduced or transmitted in any form or by any means, electronic or mechanical, including photocopying and recording, or held within any information storage and retrieval system, without permission in writing from the publisher or under licence from the Copyright Licensing Agency Limited. Further details of such licences (for reprographic reproduction) may be obtained from the Copyright Licensing Agency Limited, Saffron House, 6–10 Kirby Street, London EC1N 8TS.

Illustrations by Oxford Illustrators, Stephanie Strickland, Richard Duszczak
Layouts by Lorraine Inglis Design
Typeset in Meridien 12/14pt
Printed in Italy

A catalogue record for this title is available from the British Library

ISBN: 978 0 340 907436

Contents

Key features of *This is Geography* — 2

Unit	Your final task	
1. Living on the edge What makes Indonesia such a dangerous place to live?	Write a newspaper report about Indonesia, after the Asian tsunami	4
2. Save the rainforest! Why does it matter if the rainforest is destroyed?	Produce a guide for the Eden Project to explain why the rainforest is so important	26
3. India – a developing story Which way should India develop now?	Evaluate three different development strategies and decide which will work best for India	42
4. Food for the future What are the ingredients for a better world?	Plan a recipe so that it is good for the rest of the world, as well as for you	66
5. The Olympic Games and Paralympic Games come to town What's the secret of a successful Olympic bid?	Put together your own Olympic bid. Why would your city make a great place to host the Olympic Games?	86
6. Israel/Palestine – a land divided Is building a barrier the best way to create peace?	Decide whether building a barrier is the best way to create peace, or if there is a better option	102
7. Antarctica – the ultimate challenge Why should we be interested in Antarctica?	Make a proposal for a new scientific expedition to Antarctica	116

Key concept table — 138
Glossary — 139
Index — 141
Acknowledgements — 142

Key features of *This is Geography*

Before you start *This is Geography*, here is a quick guide to help you find your way around. Pupil's Book 3 is split into seven units, covering seven enquiries. In each one you will find the following features:

The opening spread

The unit title

Key concepts covered in this unit.

The big enquiry question – the main question you will focus on through the unit.

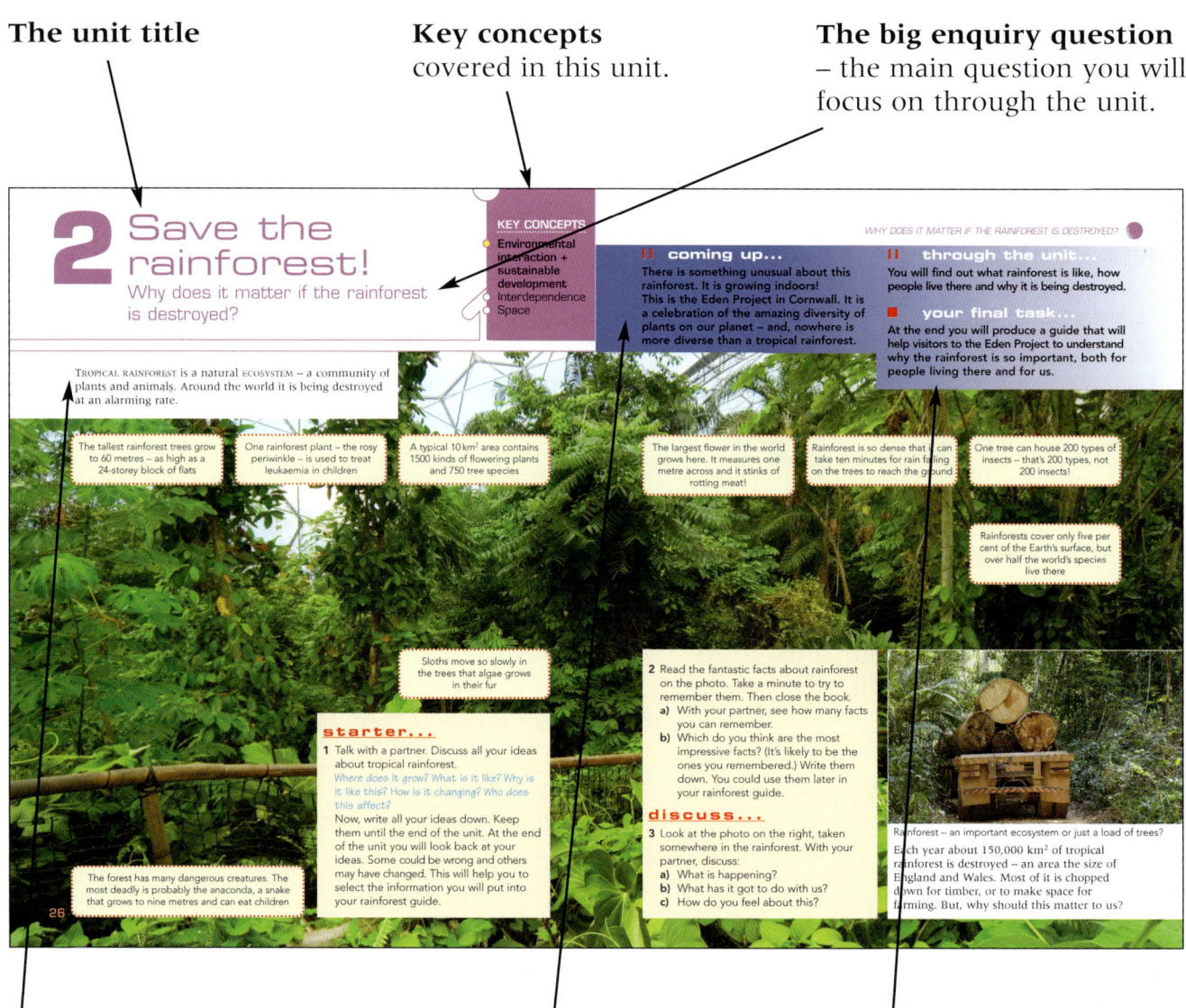

Key words – in SMALL CAPITALS. They are explained in the Glossary on pages 139–140.

Coming up – tells you what you are going to do through the rest of the unit.

Your final task – what you will be doing at the end of the enquiry to bring all your work together.

2

KEY FEATURES OF THIS IS GEOGRAPHY

Through the unit

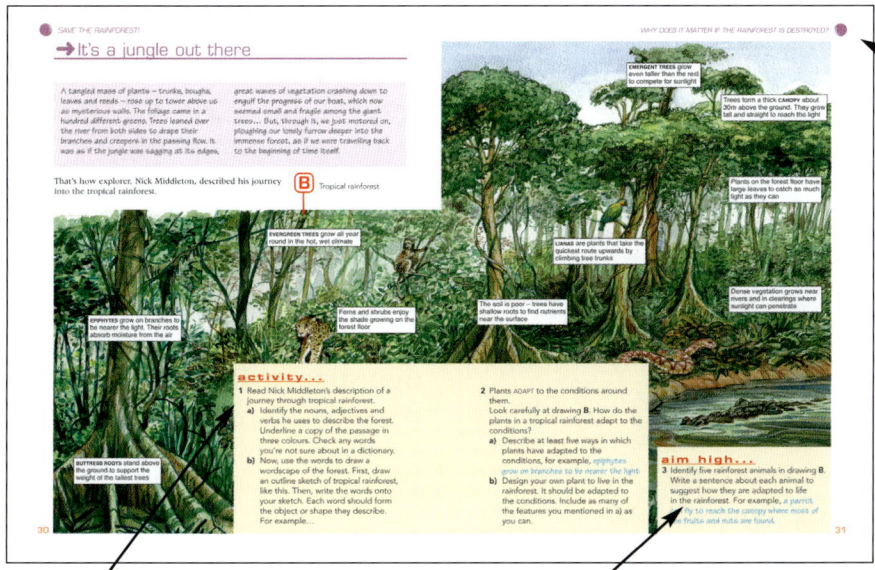

Activity – tasks that will help you to build on your enquiry, step by step.

Aim high – a challenge, and not just for the clever ones! It is a task that will help you to take your geography that little bit further.

The enquiry question – repeated on every spread so you won't forget it!

The final spread

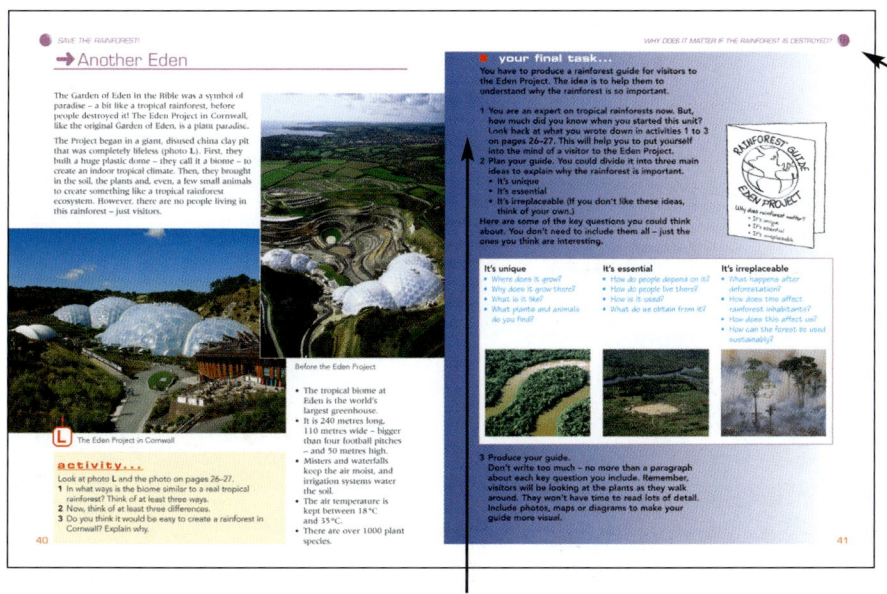

The enquiry question – again! You should know it by now.

Your final task – this is what all your work has been leading to. It is your chance to show what you know and what you can do. You may be asked to:
- draw a plan
- make a wall display
- write a story
- design a poster
- make a PowerPoint presentation.

3

1 Living on the edge

What makes Indonesia such a dangerous place to live?

KEY CONCEPT
- Physical processes
- Place
- Space

▌▌ coming up...
On December 26th 2004 the world was shocked by one of the worst ever natural disasters. A powerful earthquake off the island of Sumatra in Indonesia triggered a giant wave – or TSUNAMI. It killed over 300,000 people around the world – most of them in Indonesia.

▌▌ through the unit...
You are a journalist who sets out to report on the tsunami, but find yourself drawn into a bigger question: 'What makes Indonesia such a dangerous place to live?' As you will find out, this was not the first time that disaster has struck Indonesia, nor was it the last. Earthquakes, volcanic eruptions and tsunamis are frequent events.

▌ your final task...
At the end of the unit you will write a front page article for your newspaper.

It is 26 December 2004. You are working on the Asian desk for a British national newspaper. Reports are coming in from Indonesia of a devastating tsunami. The town of Banda Aceh in Sumatra has been destroyed.

 Banda Aceh before the tsunami

WHAT MAKES INDONESIA SUCH A DANGEROUS PLACE TO LIVE?

Banda Aceh is the capital of Aceh (say *Achai*), the northern province of Sumatra. About 320,000 people used to live there. At 8 a.m. on 26 December a major EARTHQUAKE shook the town. Buildings were badly damaged and people died, but this was nothing compared with what followed. Fifteen minutes after the earthquake, the tsunami struck. A 25-metre high wall of water swept through the city, destroying everything in its path. Half of Banda Aceh's population were killed and the rest became homeless.

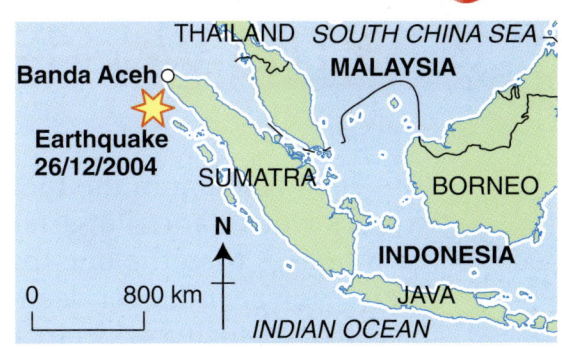

B Banda Aceh after the tsunami

starter...

1 Look at photo **A**.
   a) Try to identify each of these features in the photo:

   > the sea   a beach   trees   roads
   > houses   bridges   fishing boats

   b) From what you can see, try to describe the sort of place Banda Aceh is. Write two or three sentences. Your first sentence could start like this, *Banda Aceh lies on the coast of Sumatra...*

2 Now, look at photo **B**. Compare it with photo **A**.
   Describe carefully what has happened to each of the features you identified in **A**. For example, *One of the bridges has been destroyed.*

aim high...

3 You are one of the first journalists to arrive in Banda Aceh after the tsunami. Imagine what it would be like on the ground. Send a report back to your newspaper to describe the impact of the tsunami. Use the photos on this spread to help you.

LIVING ON THE EDGE

➡ The world's worst disaster?

The 2004 tsunami in the Indian Ocean was probably the world's worst natural disaster. There have been bigger earthquakes than the one that caused the tsunami, and there have been higher death tolls, but no previous disaster has affected such a wide area, killing so many people in different countries at the same time.

investigate...

Your editor asks you to investigate the question 'What makes Indonesia such a dangerous place to live?' The tsunami is the latest in a long list of disasters to hit Indonesia. Through the rest of the unit, make notes to help you to write your article. As you do this, list any photos, maps or diagrams you could use.

Start your notes now. Complete the sentences below to explain why Indonesia was so badly affected by the tsunami. For example, *The earthquake measured 9.0 on the Richter Scale, one of the most powerful earthquakes ever recorded.*

- The earthquake measured 9.0 on the Richter scale…
- The earthquake happened close to Indonesia…
- The coast of Sumatra is low-lying…
- There was no early warning system for tsunamis in the Indian Ocean…

aim high...

a) Complete a table like the one below. List all the countries affected by the tsunami.

Country	Time for tsunami to reach	Wave height	Number of deaths
Indonesia	15 minutes	25 m	230,000

b) Describe the pattern in your table.
c) How can you explain the pattern?

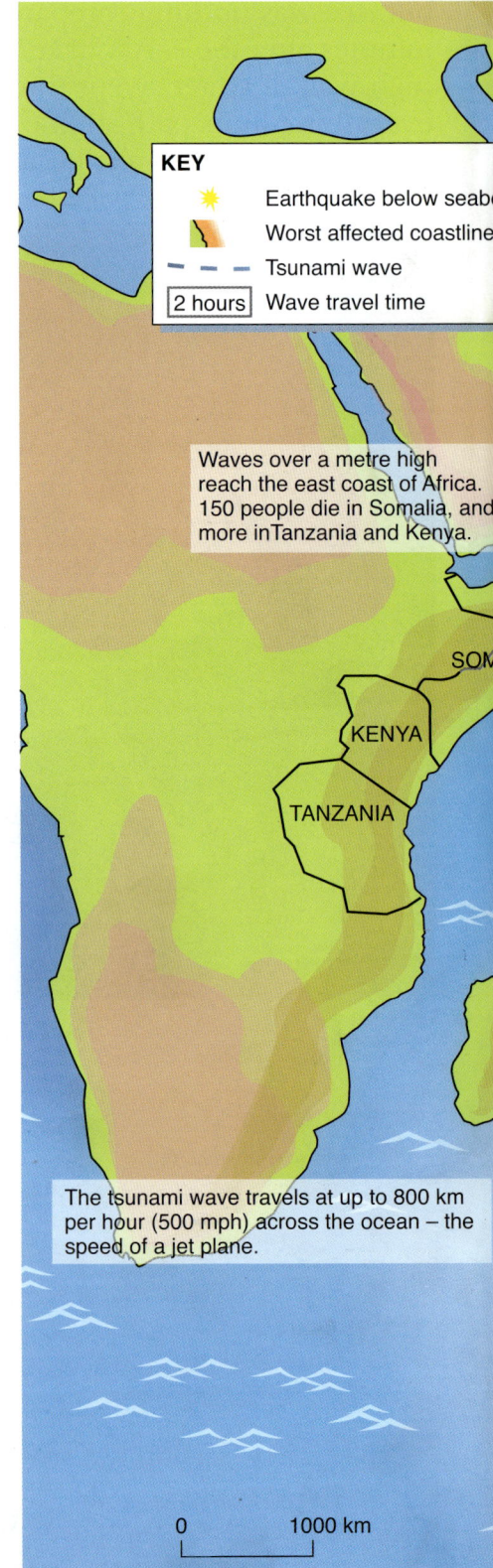

The Indian Ocean tsunami, 26 December 2004 **D**

WHAT MAKES INDONESIA SUCH A DANGEROUS PLACE TO LIVE?

The tsunami hits the coast of Thailand, 400 km from the earthquake **C**

Waves up to 12 metres high hit the coast of Sri Lanka. 1,000 people drown on a train hit by the wave. Altogether, 38,000 people are killed in Sri Lanka, and a further 16,000 in India.

The wave takes an hour to reach the coast of Thailand. About 12,000 people die, many of them European tourists on their Christmas holiday.

A wave up to 25 metres high (like a 10-storey block of flats) hits the low-lying coast of Sumatra in Indonesia 15 minutes after the earthquake. Up to 230,000 people are killed.

Waves up to five metres high hit the tiny Maldives islands and kill about 80 people.

The earthquake that triggers the tsunami happens here, deep under the sea floor, at 7:58 a.m. It measures 9.0 on the Richter Scale, one of the most powerful ever recorded.

There is no early warning system for tsunamis in the Indian Ocean, so countries are not prepared.

The tsunami also hits Australia, South Africa and Antarctica. It even crosses the Pacific Ocean to reach the west coast of America. There are no reports of any deaths.

7

LIVING ON THE EDGE

→ The shock wave

Tsunamis are the most dramatic and destructive waves. They can be triggered by anything that disturbs the sea floor, such as a major earthquake or volcanic eruption. The bigger the disturbance, the bigger the tsunami will be.

activity...

1. Look at the drawings in **E**. Describe the experience of a tsunami for:
   a) a passenger in a boat far out at sea
   b) a person in a hotel on the coast.
   Mention what happens before, during and after.

E What happens in a tsunami

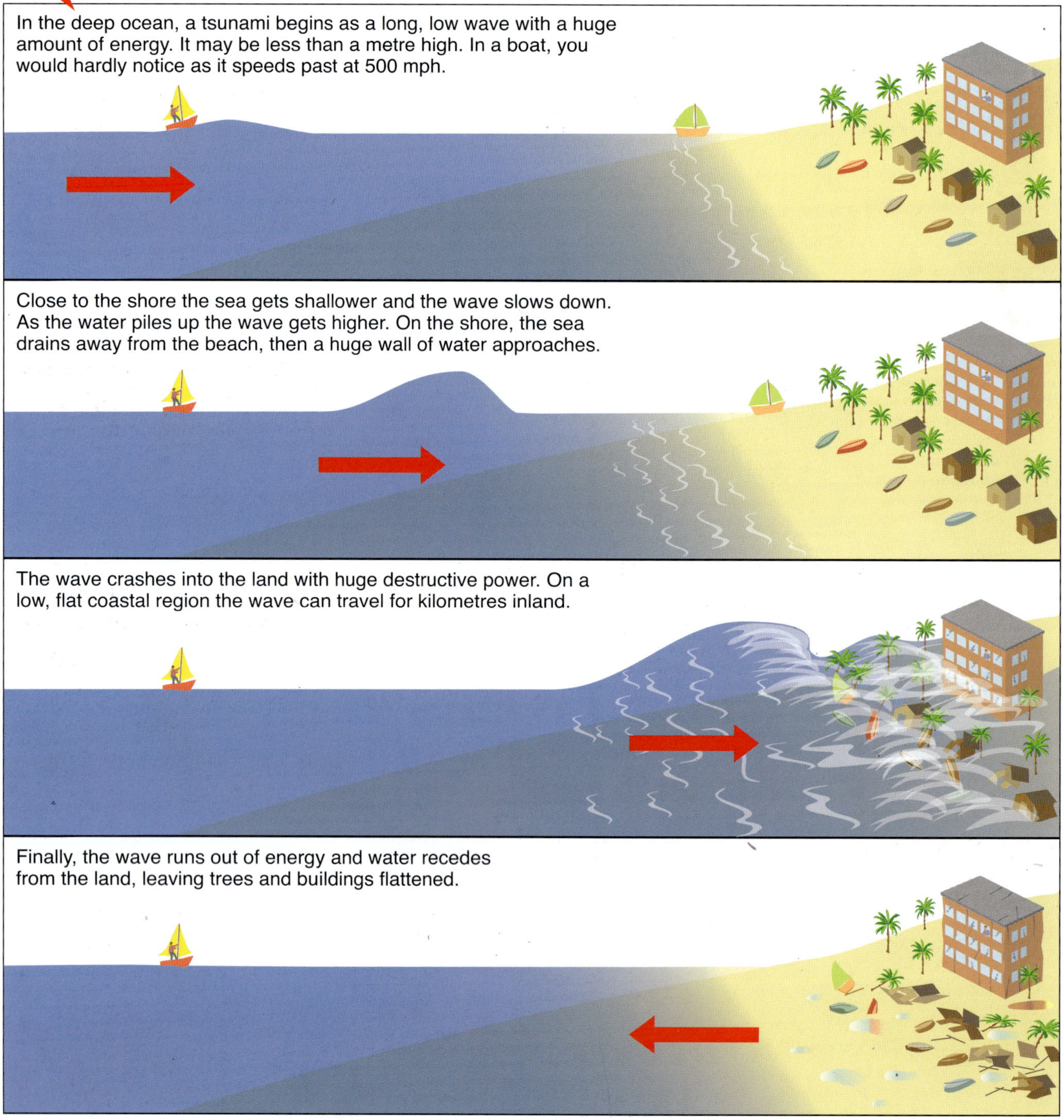

In the deep ocean, a tsunami begins as a long, low wave with a huge amount of energy. It may be less than a metre high. In a boat, you would hardly notice as it speeds past at 500 mph.

Close to the shore the sea gets shallower and the wave slows down. As the water piles up the wave gets higher. On the shore, the sea drains away from the beach, then a huge wall of water approaches.

The wave crashes into the land with huge destructive power. On a low, flat coastal region the wave can travel for kilometres inland.

Finally, the wave runs out of energy and water recedes from the land, leaving trees and buildings flattened.

WHAT MAKES INDONESIA SUCH A DANGEROUS PLACE TO LIVE?

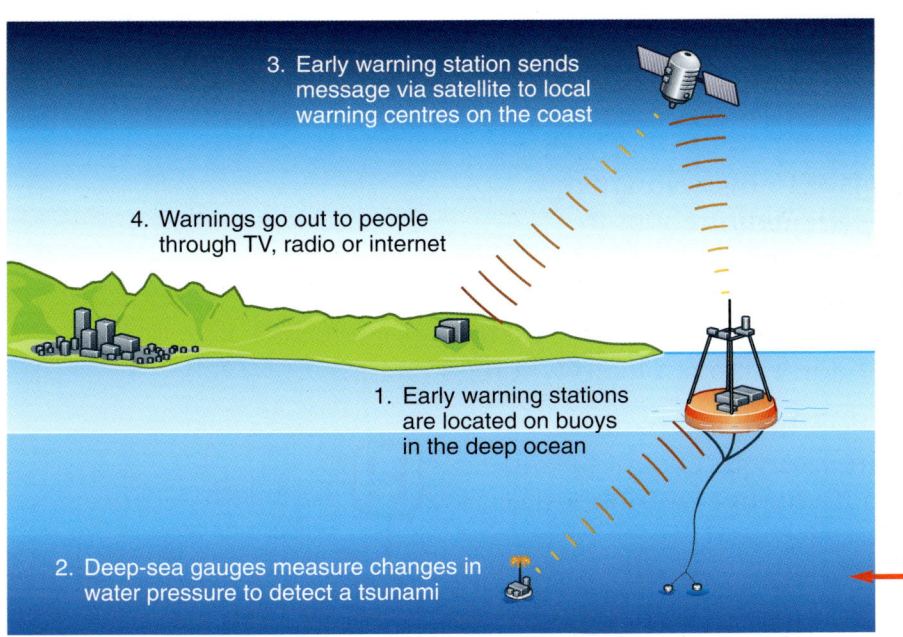

Countries around the Pacific Ocean are prepared for tsunamis. They have set up an early warning system to detect tsunamis before they reach land. There was no early warning system for the Indian Ocean in 2004.

F How a tsunami early warning system works

2 Study drawing **F**.
Explain how an early warning system could have helped to reduce deaths from the Indian Ocean tsunami.

aim high...

3 Look at the data in table **G**.
  a) What differences in wealth do you notice between countries around the Pacific and Indian oceans?
  b) How could this explain why the Pacific Ocean has a tsunami early warning system and the Indian Ocean doesn't?
  c) In what other ways could wealth affect countries' ability to respond to natural hazards, like tsunamis or earthquakes? (You will find out how Indonesia responded to an earthquake on pages 18–19.)

investigate...

Make more notes to help you to write your article. Remember, you have to investigate the question *What makes Indonesia such a dangerous place to live?*

Parts of your notes have gone missing. Complete the notes below.
- *Tsunamis are dramatic and destructive. They are caused by...*
- *People have little time to prepare for tsunamis. The first warning...*
- *The Pacific Ocean has a tsunami early warning system. This helps countries...*
- *The Indian Ocean has no early warning system. As a result...*

Countries around the Pacific Ocean	GDP (wealth) per person $
Canada	28,930
Chile	9,420
Japan	27,380
Russian Federation	8,080
USA	36,110
Countries around the Indian Ocean	GDP (wealth) per person $
India	2,650
Indonesia	3,070
Somalia	600
Sri Lanka	3,510
Thailand	6,890

G Wealth around the Pacific Ocean and the Indian Ocean

LIVING ON THE EDGE

→ It's a dangerous world

The world can be a dangerous place to live. Nowhere is completely safe, but some places are definitely more hazardous than others. Let's look at two of the most deadly NATURAL HAZARDS: earthquakes and volcanoes. In an average year they kill thousands of people worldwide, and make many more people homeless. Yet, they don't happen everywhere.

Look at map **H** and you will notice there is a pattern. For example, you are much more likely to experience an earthquake or volcanic eruption if you live in Indonesia, than if you live in the UK.

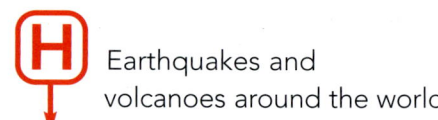

Earthquakes and volcanoes around the world

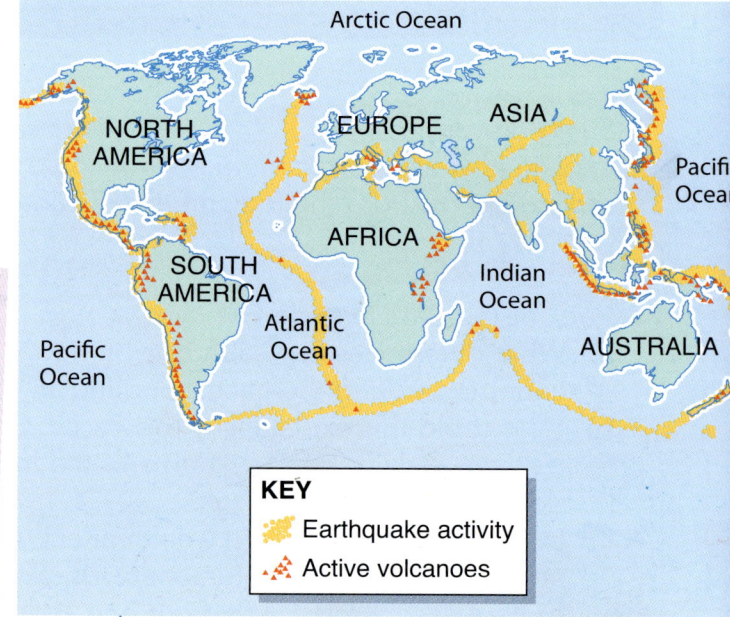

activity...

1 Look carefully at map **H**. Notice the pattern of earthquakes and volcanoes.
 a) Read these statements. Choose three that are true.

> Earthquakes and volcanoes happen everywhere
>
> Earthquakes and volcanoes often happen in the same places
>
> Earthquakes and volcanoes happen in the ocean as well as on land
>
> Earthquakes and volcanoes only happen in hot countries
>
> Earthquakes and volcanoes happen mainly on large continents
>
> Earthquakes and volcanoes occur along lines

 b) Describe the pattern on the map, using the statements you chose. You can add more sentences of your own.
2 Earthquakes and volcanic eruptions are happening all the time. Do some internet research into earthquakes and volcanic eruptions that have occurred in the past week.

Use these two websites to do your research: National Earthquake Information Centre at http://earthquake.usgs.gov. Click on 'Latest earthquakes' University of North Dakota's Volcano World at http://volcano.und.edu. Click on 'Current eruptions'
 a) Mark and label places where these earthquakes and eruptions have occurred on a world map. Show at least ten. Were there any earthquakes or eruptions in Indonesia?
 b) Compare your map with map **H**. What do you notice?

WHAT MAKES INDONESIA SUCH A DANGEROUS PLACE TO LIVE?

Indonesia is a country with a population of about 240 million living on 13,000 islands. Many of the islands are volcanic. Altogether, there are 76 active volcanoes, more than any other country (map **I**). Indonesia also suffers from frequent earthquakes.

Many of Indonesia's mountains are volcanoes

I Active volcanoes in Indonesia

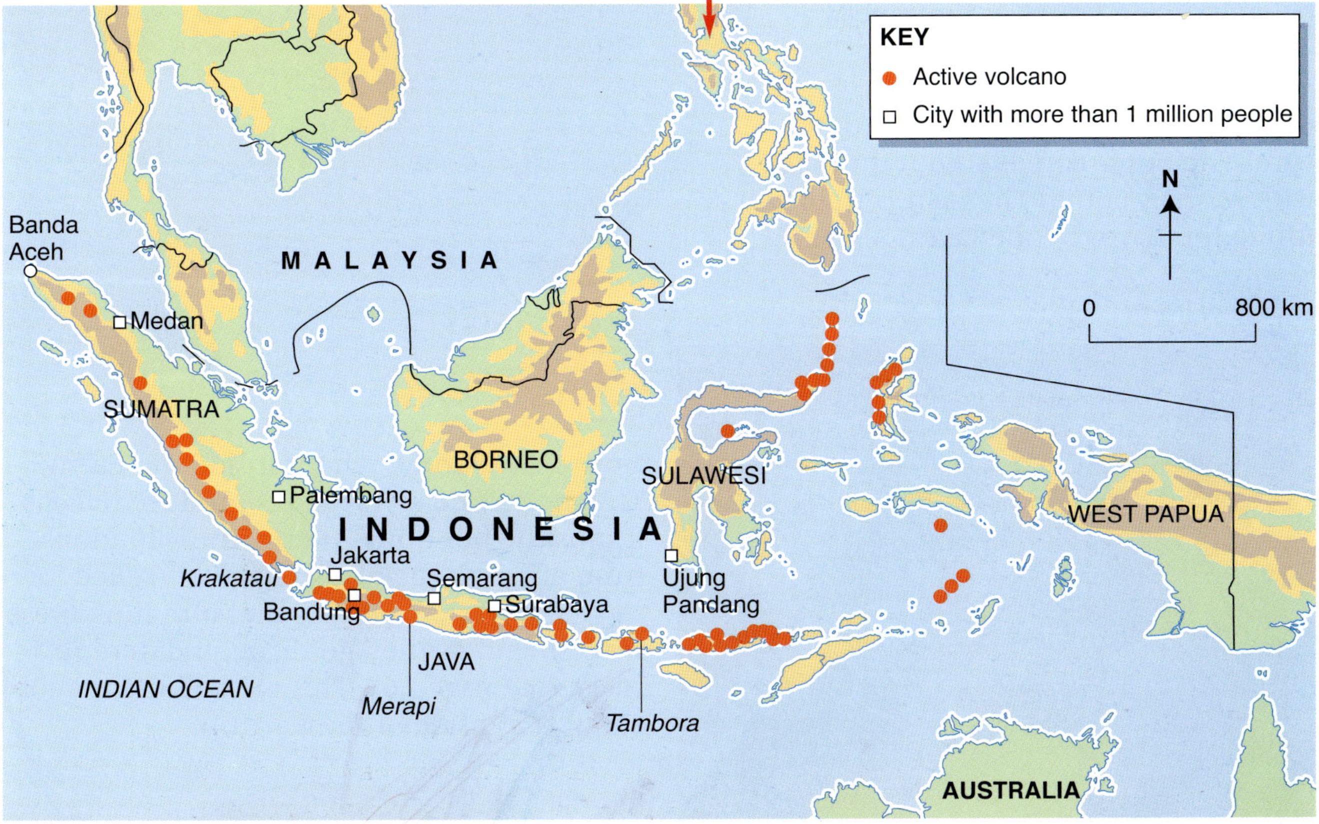

aim high...

3 Look carefully at map **I**. Even in Indonesia some places are more dangerous than others.
   a) Describe the distribution of volcanoes in Indonesia. Mention the islands where volcanoes are found.
   b) Where are most of the largest cities? Why could this be dangerous?

investigate...

Make more notes to help you to write your article. Remember, you have to investigate the question: 'What makes Indonesia such a dangerous place to live?'
Here are some words to include in your notes:

natural hazards   volcanoes   islands
pattern   earthquakes   cities   Java

LIVING ON THE EDGE

→ Going deeper

The reasons that earthquakes and volcanoes occur are found deep within the Earth.

You can think of the Earth like an apple.
- The bit that we live on is the skin. It is a thin layer of solid rock called the CRUST. It is thicker under the land than it is under the ocean.
- Below the crust lies the MANTLE. It is a much thicker layer of rock that, as you go deeper, gets so hot it behaves like a liquid. It flows very slowly like extra thick treacle.
- Further down still is the CORE: divided into the inner core and outer core. The outer core is so hot that the rock *really* is liquid. The heat is trapped inside the Earth by the layers above.

Lava flow from a volcano

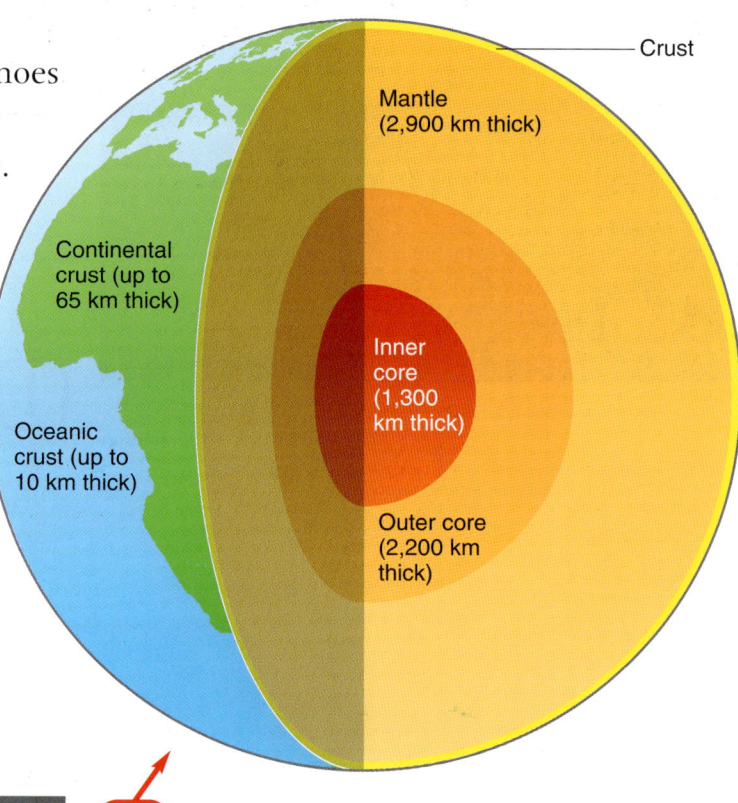

J Inside the Earth

How do we know what's inside the Earth? The molten rock volcanoes produce tells us it must be hot down there! The vibrations from an earthquake also help us (called SEISMIC WAVES). Scientists measure how these waves bend as they go through different rocks (see page 16). This can tell them a lot about the inside of the Earth.

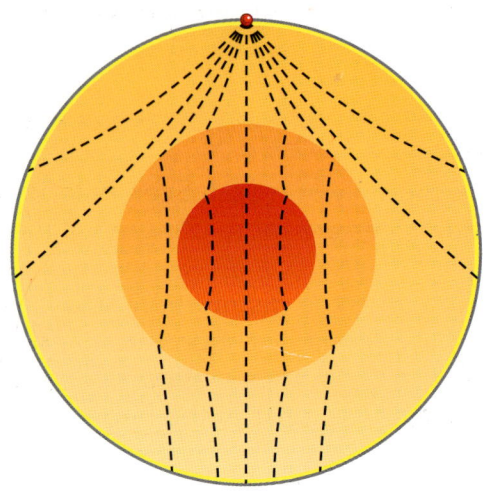

Seismic waves from an earthquake

WHAT MAKES INDONESIA SUCH A DANGEROUS PLACE TO LIVE?

The Earth's crust is cracked, like an eggshell, into enormous pieces, called PLATES. Some plates cover whole continents or oceans, but others are much smaller (map **K**). They float on the mantle below and are continuously moving around – just a few centimetres every year. It is along these cracks – or PLATE BOUNDARIES – that earthquakes and volcanoes are most likely to occur.

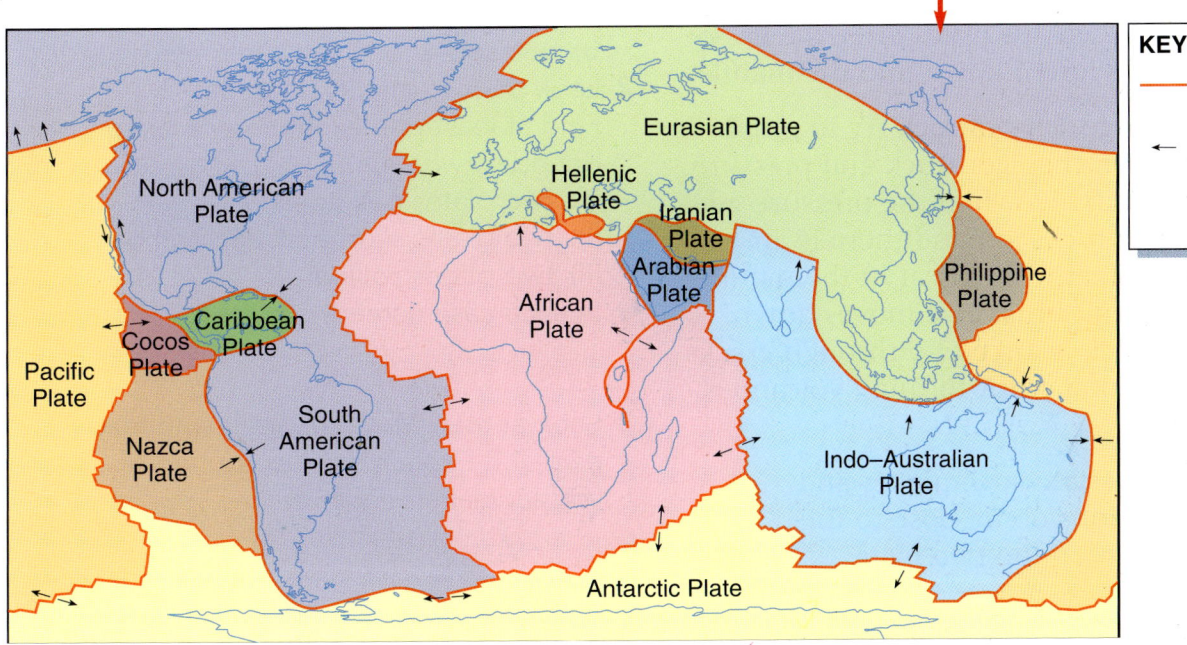

K The Earth's plates

KEY
— Plate boundary
← Direction in which plate is moving

activity...

1. Look at drawing **J**. Use it to help you draw a cross-section of the Earth, like this.
   a) Choose a suitable scale to fit the cross-section on your page, for example 1 cm : 1,000 km.
   b) Draw the cross-section with a compass. Make each layer the correct depth.
   c) Label your cross-section.

2. Look very carefully at map **K**. You are going to make your own jigsaw map of the Earth. Your teacher will give you a sheet with all the jigsaw pieces on.
   a) Close the book after you have looked at the map.
   b) Cut out the pieces from your sheet. Try to put them together from memory to make the map.
   c) Stick the pieces down in your book. Give the map a title.

3. Compare map **K** with map **H**, on page 10.
   a) Write a sentence to describe what you see.
   b) Which plates do i) Indonesia, and ii) the UK, lie on? How close is each country to a plate boundary?

aim high...

4. Suggest your own theory to explain why, a) earthquakes, and b) volcanoes, often occur at plate boundaries. You can check your theory on page 14.

investigate...

Make more notes to help you to write your article. Remember, you have to investigate the question: 'What makes Indonesia such a dangerous place to live?'

LIVING ON THE EDGE

➡ Plates under pressure

Indonesia lies close to the boundary between two plates. The OCEANIC CRUST of the Indian Plate is moving slowly towards the CONTINENTAL CRUST of the Eurasian Plate (drawing **L**). Where the plates meet, the heavy oceanic crust is forced down into the mantle.

As the two huge slabs of rock try to grind past each other, they get stuck and pressure builds up. Suddenly, when the pressure gets too much, the rocks jolt and there is an earthquake. Meanwhile, heat in the mantle melts the oceanic crust as it moves down. The molten rock is forced up through cracks in the continental crust, forming volcanoes at the surface.

Most of Indonesia's earthquakes and volcanic eruptions occur close to the boundary between the two plates.

activity...

1. Look at cross-section **L**.
   Explain why, a) earthquakes, and
   b) volcanoes, occur at the plate boundary.
2. Look back at map **K** on page 13.
   Find at least one example of a plate boundary where:
   i) two plates pull apart
   ii) two plates slide past each other
   iii) two plates collide
   In each case name the plates.

aim high...

3. Look at map **M**. Compare it with map **I** on page 11. Explain the distribution of volcanoes in Indonesia.

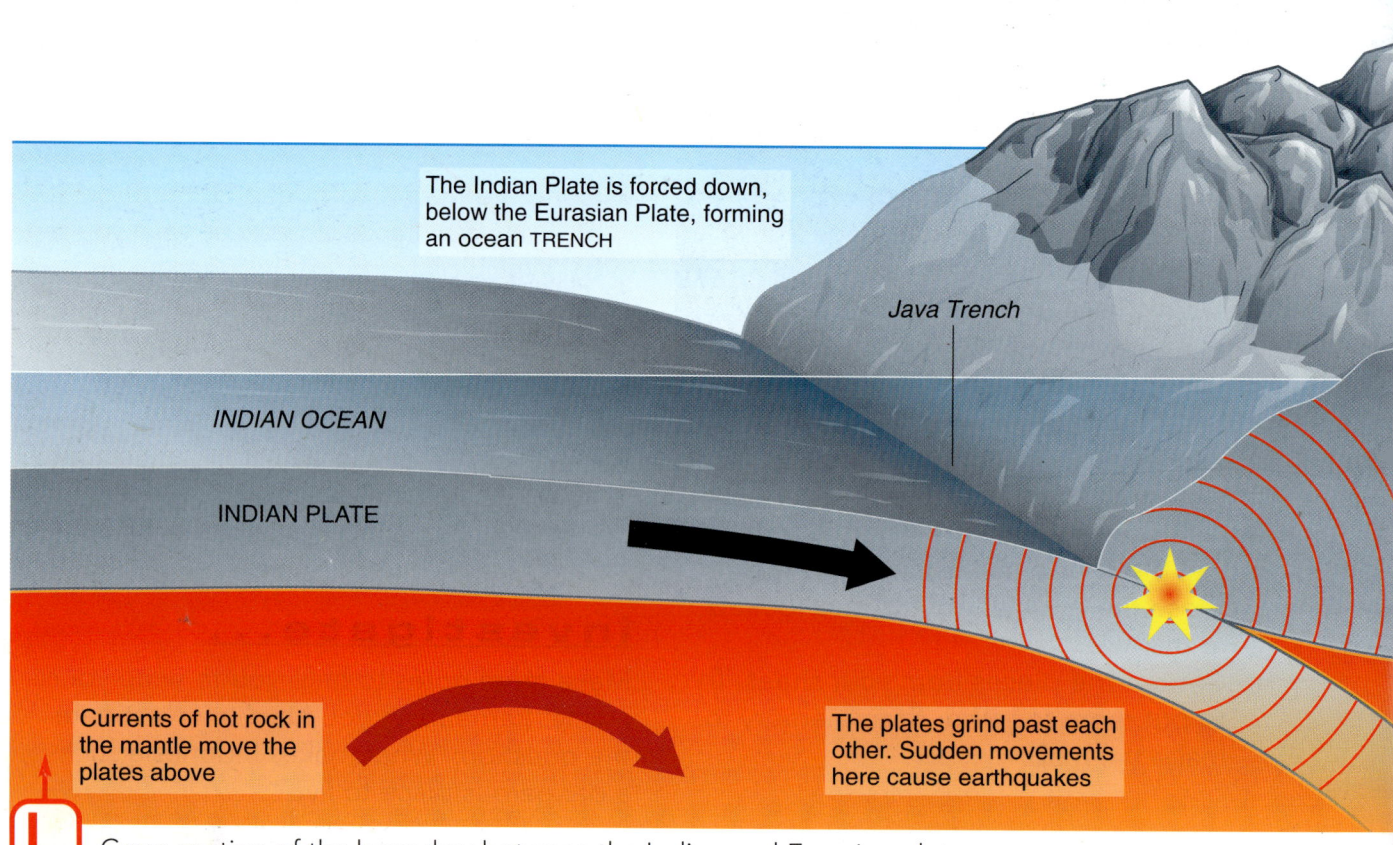

L Cross-section of the boundary between the Indian and Eurasian plates

WHAT MAKES INDONESIA SUCH A DANGEROUS PLACE TO LIVE?

investigate...

Make more notes to help you to write your article. Remember, you have to investigate the question: 'What makes Indonesia such a dangerous place to live?'

M Map of Indonesia showing plate boundaries

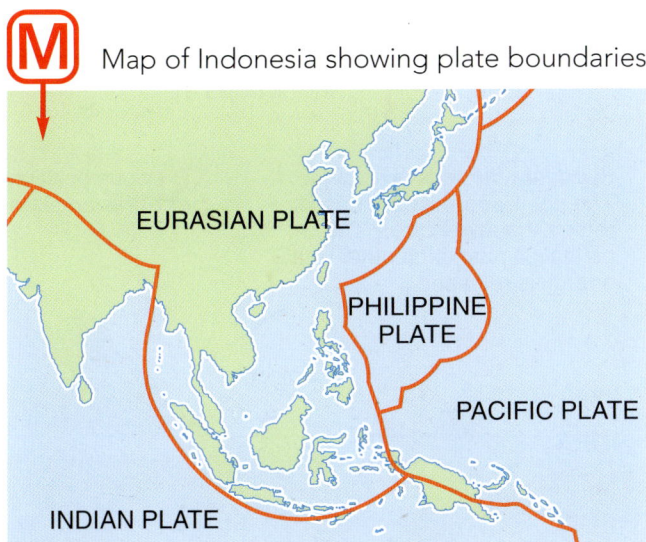

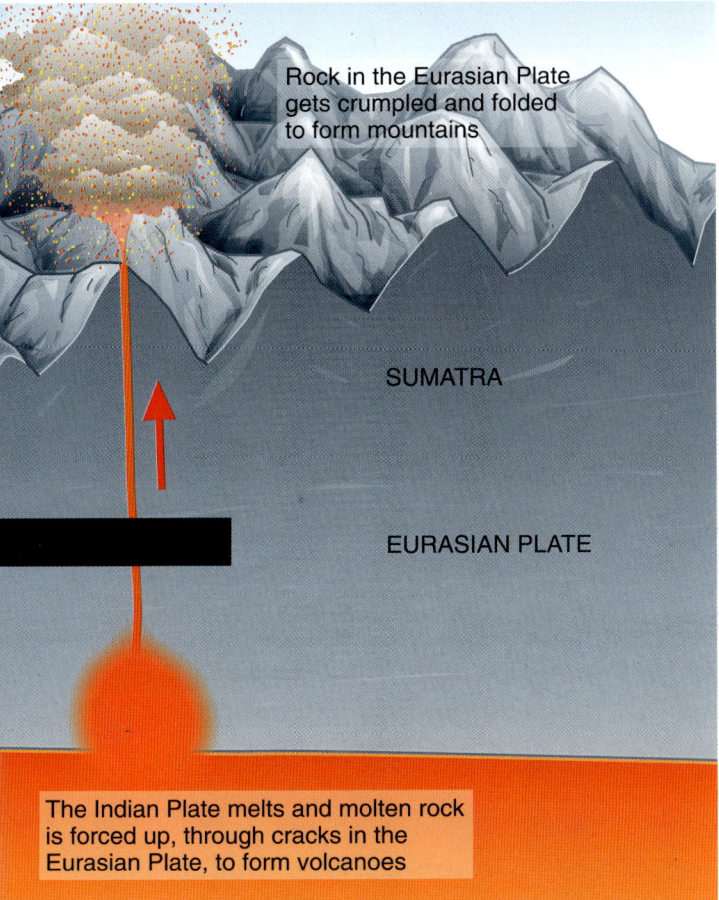

Rock in the Eurasian Plate gets crumpled and folded to form mountains

SUMATRA

EURASIAN PLATE

The Indian Plate melts and molten rock is forced up, through cracks in the Eurasian Plate, to form volcanoes

Other types of plate boundary

1. **Plates pull apart**

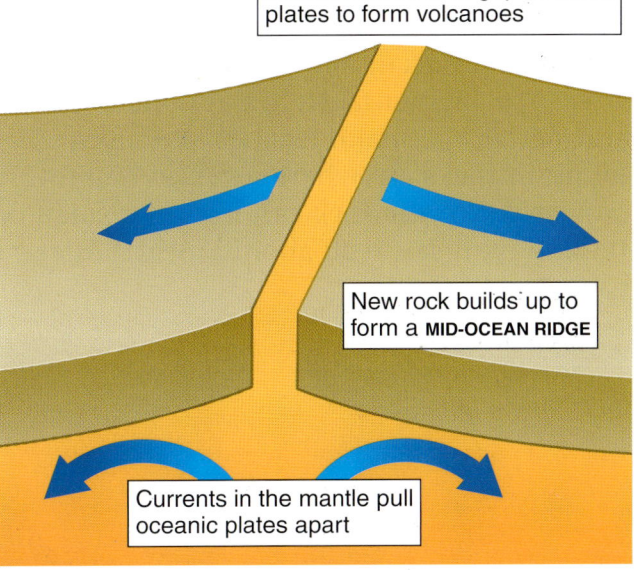

Molten rock rises in gap between plates to form volcanoes

New rock builds up to form a MID-OCEAN RIDGE

Currents in the mantle pull oceanic plates apart

2. **Plates slide past each other**

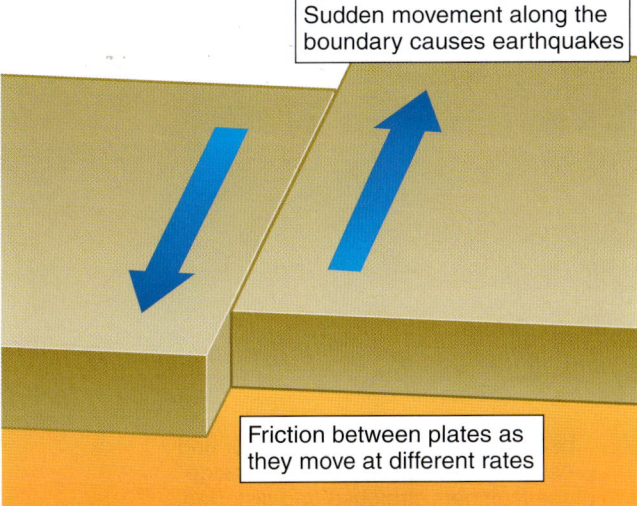

Sudden movement along the boundary causes earthquakes

Friction between plates as they move at different rates

3. **Plates collide**

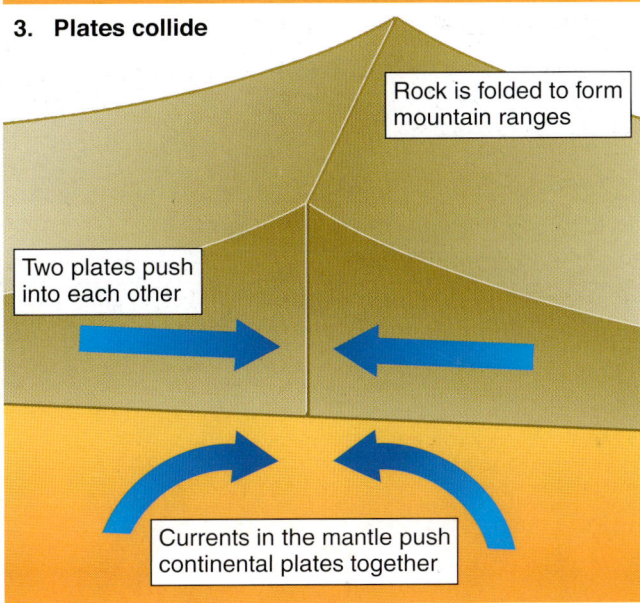

Rock is folded to form mountain ranges

Two plates push into each other

Currents in the mantle push continental plates together

15

LIVING ON THE EDGE

→ Earthquakes

Earthquakes occur along FAULTS, or cracks, in the Earth's crust. The biggest faults are at plate boundaries, and that's also where the major earthquakes occur. Faults can be found in rocks anywhere, even in Britain. A slight movement in the rock can lead to a small earthquake or TREMOR (you can read about an earthquake in Britain on page 24).

What causes earthquakes in Indonesia?

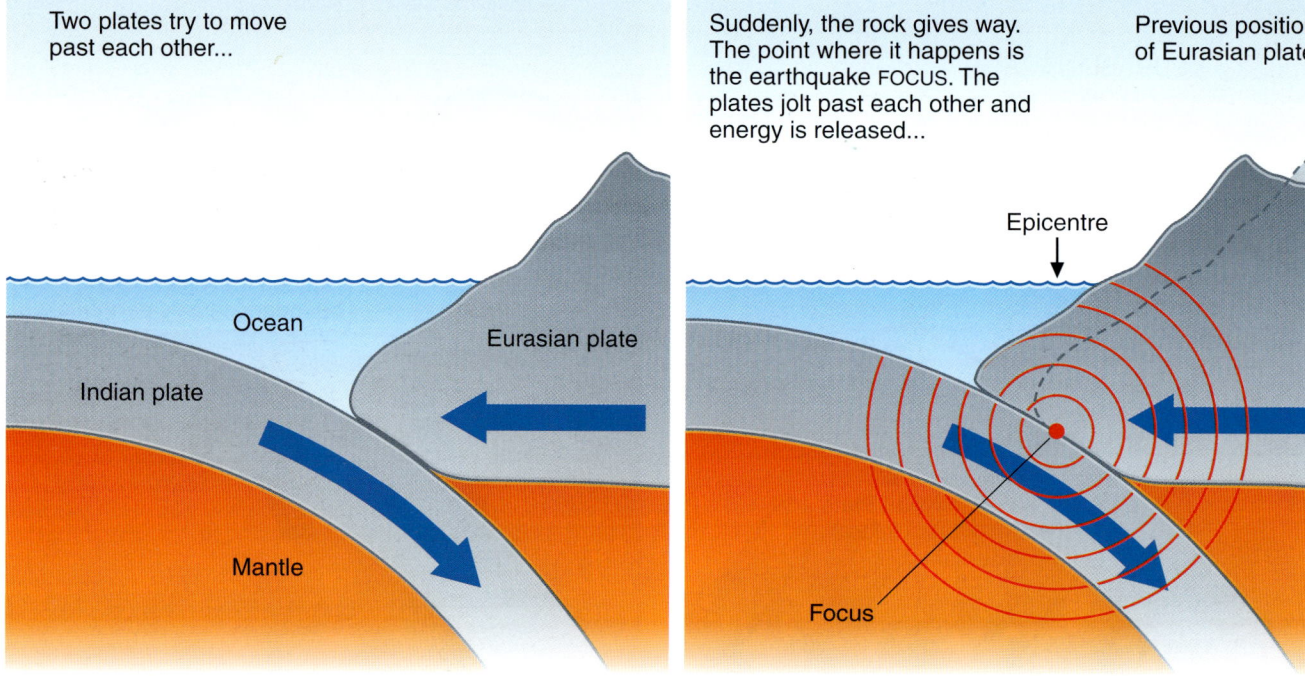

Two plates try to move past each other...

...but the plates get locked together and pressure builds up. Rock on either side of the fault gets stretched and distorted.

Suddenly, the rock gives way. The point where it happens is the earthquake FOCUS. The plates jolt past each other and energy is released...

...sending seismic waves through the rock. The point above the focus, where the earthquake is felt most strongly, is the EPICENTRE.

The closer the earthquake is to the surface the stronger it will be felt. Like ripples on a pond, the seismic waves get weaker the further they travel through the rock. The amount of energy released in an earthquake is measured on the RICHTER SCALE.

A SEISMOGRAPH is an instrument used to record the seismic waves from an earthquake

WHAT MAKES INDONESIA SUCH A DANGEROUS PLACE TO LIVE?

The Richter Scale

↑ INCREASING ENERGY

OVER 9
Only five earthquakes this big have been recorded since 1900.

9
Great earthquake. Leads to widespread damage over an area hundreds of kilometres across. The earthquake that triggered the tsunami on 26th December, 2004 measured 9.

8
Major earthquake. Causes serious damage over an area tens of kilometres across. Buildings and bridges topple. At sea it may trigger a tsunami.

7
Strong tremors felt across a wide area. In cities people may run out of building in panic. Poorly-designed buildings may collapse.

6
Tremors may damage poorly-designed buildings.

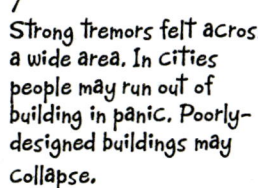
I've been meaning to do something about that roof for ages!

5
Windows and doors rattle. Small objects fall over.

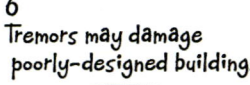
Did you feel that?
Did someone fall out of bed?

4
Vibrations can be felt.

3
You would not feel an earthquake this small, but it would be recorded on a seismograph!

2

1

activity...

1 Study these pages carefully. Find the correct word to match these meanings.

★ a crack in the Earth's crust
★ the origin of an earthquake
★ the point on the surface above an earthquake
★ a small earthquake
★ an instrument used to record earthquakes
★ the scale that measures an earthquake's strength

2 You are given these materials. How could you use them to make a model showing what happens in an earthquake?

block of wood   heavy weight   elastic band

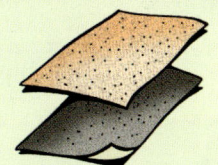 

two pieces of sandpaper   some pins

a) Suggest how you could make an earthquake model.
b) Explain how your model works and how it shows what happens in an earthquake. If you have the right materials, you could try making your model at home.

aim high...

3 Go back to the National Earthquake Information Centre website at http://earthquake.usgs.gov
  a) Find out more about an earthquake in Indonesia. What did it measure on the Richter Scale?
  b) Describe the damage caused by the earthquake.

A second strike

On 28 March 2005, just three months after the Indian Ocean tsunami, another major earthquake struck Indonesia. It happened on the same fault, at the boundary between the Indian and Eurasian plates. This time the epicentre was on the small island of Nias, off the coast of Sumatra, south of the earlier earthquake (map **P**).

The second earthquake measured 8.7 on the Richter Scale. Over a thousand people were killed as buildings collapsed on top of them. Tremors were felt as far away as Singapore and Thailand. But this time, there was no tsunami.

Scientists had predicted the earthquake. The earthquake in December put more stress on rock further along the fault. It is normal to get a series of AFTERSHOCKS, as the rock readjusts after a major earthquake.

0 500 km
SOUTH CHINA SEA
MALAYSIA
Banda Aceh
26/12/04
N
Nias
28/03/05
SUMATRA
INDIAN OCEAN
Java Trench
Jakarta
KEY
Earthquake
Plate boundary

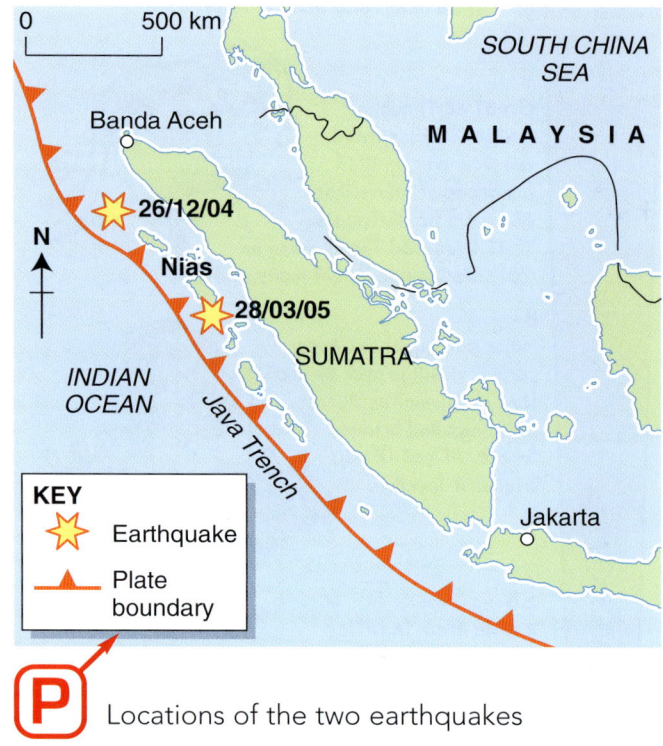

P Locations of the two earthquakes

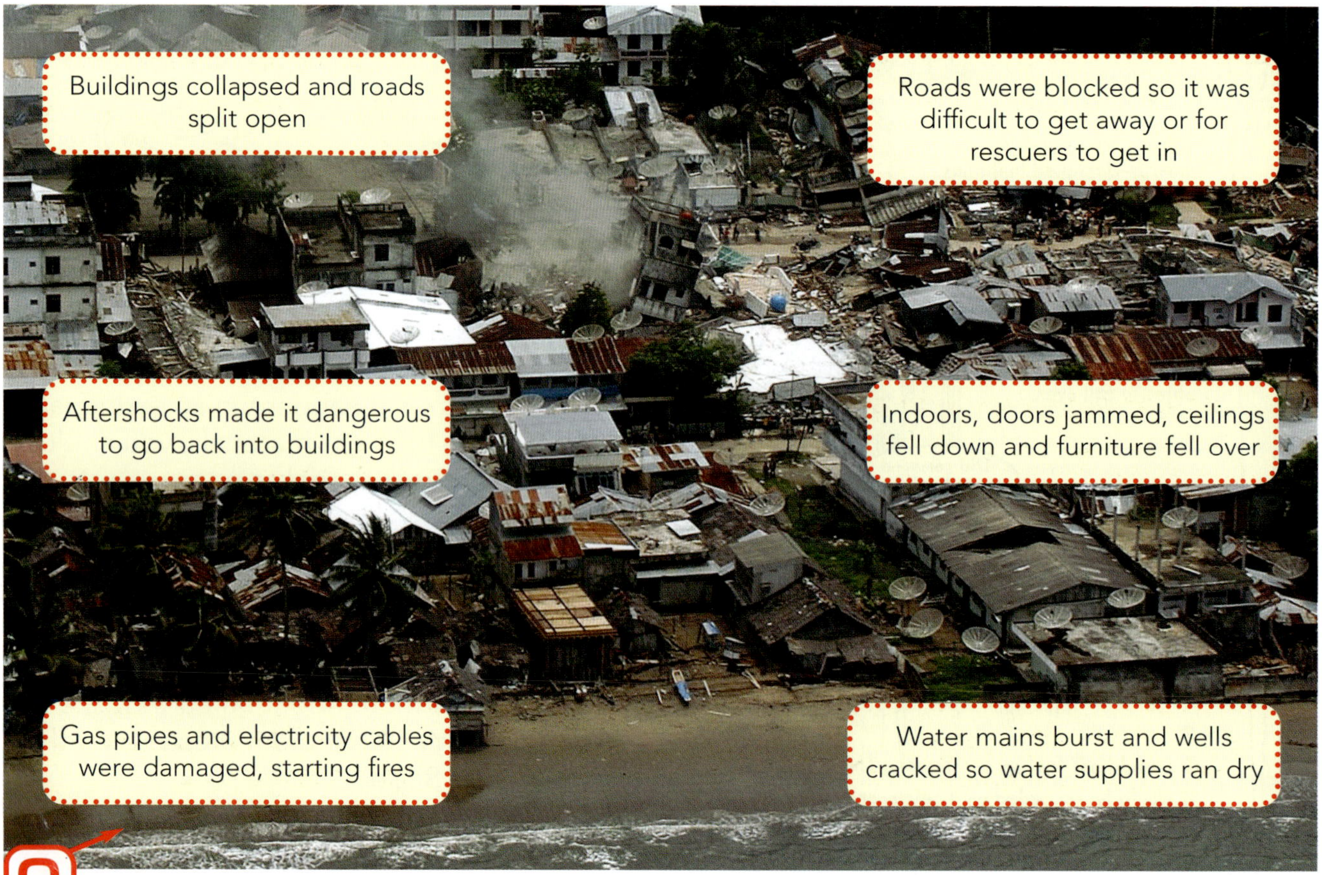

Buildings collapsed and roads split open
Roads were blocked so it was difficult to get away or for rescuers to get in
Aftershocks made it dangerous to go back into buildings
Indoors, doors jammed, ceilings fell down and furniture fell over
Gas pipes and electricity cables were damaged, starting fires
Water mains burst and wells cracked so water supplies ran dry

Q Earthquake damage in Nias

WHAT MAKES INDONESIA SUCH A DANGEROUS PLACE TO LIVE?

Usnaya Sahib who lives on Nias lost her home and livelihood on 28th March. She was interviewed a few days later, living in a temporary shelter with her husband and three children.

Usnaya Sahib and her husband, Muklihun, were in their house when it began to shake. They grabbed their children and tried to get out, but the door had jammed. They had no choice but to wait.

The shaking got worse and pieces of the roof started to fall on top of them. 'Allahu Akbar (God is great)', they shouted.

Then one of the walls fell and they escaped; they were lucky they lived in a wooden house. The ground was still shaking, and cracks in the street were opening up around their feet, so they ran towards the hills, aware that a giant wave could come at any time from the sea. Muklihun had to carry his son Dio, because he has polio.

Many people ran to the hills. They all spoke of the approaching giant wave, like the one in Aceh. The family ran on. It was dark. They lost their shoes, and continued on bare feet. They stayed in the mountains for two nights, with little to eat and water only from natural springs. No-one came to help. After several days they came down from the mountains. Being Muslims, on Friday they go to the mosque. Oxfam were there, providing water and food. The family was very grateful.

They were shocked and upset by the remains of their home, which was now a pile of rubble and wood, with the smell of death all around. Luckily, the well still worked. There was a lot of sad news. Their pregnant neighbour and friend was killed, as well as her young son.

Muklihun's beca (bicycle taxi) – upon which the family's livelihood depended – was broken and could not be repaired. They had borrowed the money to buy it, and that money still has to be paid back. They cannot afford to pay school fees. Nias is a poor place, and most of the men go to Sumatra (the mainland 150 km away) to find work.

Usnaya says, 'I have to accept what has happened. I try to smile and laugh; it is the way to look young. And I can smile tonight because my family will eat rice.'

activity...

1 Look at map **P**.
   a) Write a paragraph to describe the location of the epicentre of the earthquake on 28 March. Mention each of these features in your paragraph.

   Indian Ocean   Nias   Sumatra
   epicentre of 26 December earthquake
   Indian/Eurasian plate boundary

   b) Explain the connection between the two earthquakes.

2 Study photo **Q** and read the account of the earthquake. Imagine you work for Oxfam. You are in charge of relief work in Nias after the earthquake.
   a) What help will people need in the days and weeks after the earthquake? Make a list of the priorities. Mention at least five. For example,

   clean, safe water supply

   b) What help will people need during the next year? Make a list of at least five more.

aim high...

3 Indonesia is a fairly poor country. How will this affect its ability to recover from the earthquake? (Look at your responses in activity 2 for ideas.)

investigate...

Make more notes to help you to write your article. Look back at the last four pages (16–19) to make your notes. You have to investigate the question: 'What makes Indonesia such a dangerous place to live?'

LIVING ON THE EDGE

→ Volcano

A VOLCANO is an opening in the Earth's crust where MAGMA (molten rock deep below ground) erupts at the surface. Volcanoes come in different shapes and sizes, but a typical volcano is a steep-sided mountain built up from layers of ASH and LAVA from previous eruptions.

Most of the world's volcanoes are found near plate boundaries. One of these is Merapi on the island of Java in Indonesia (**R**).

 Cross-section of Merapi, a volcano in Indonesia

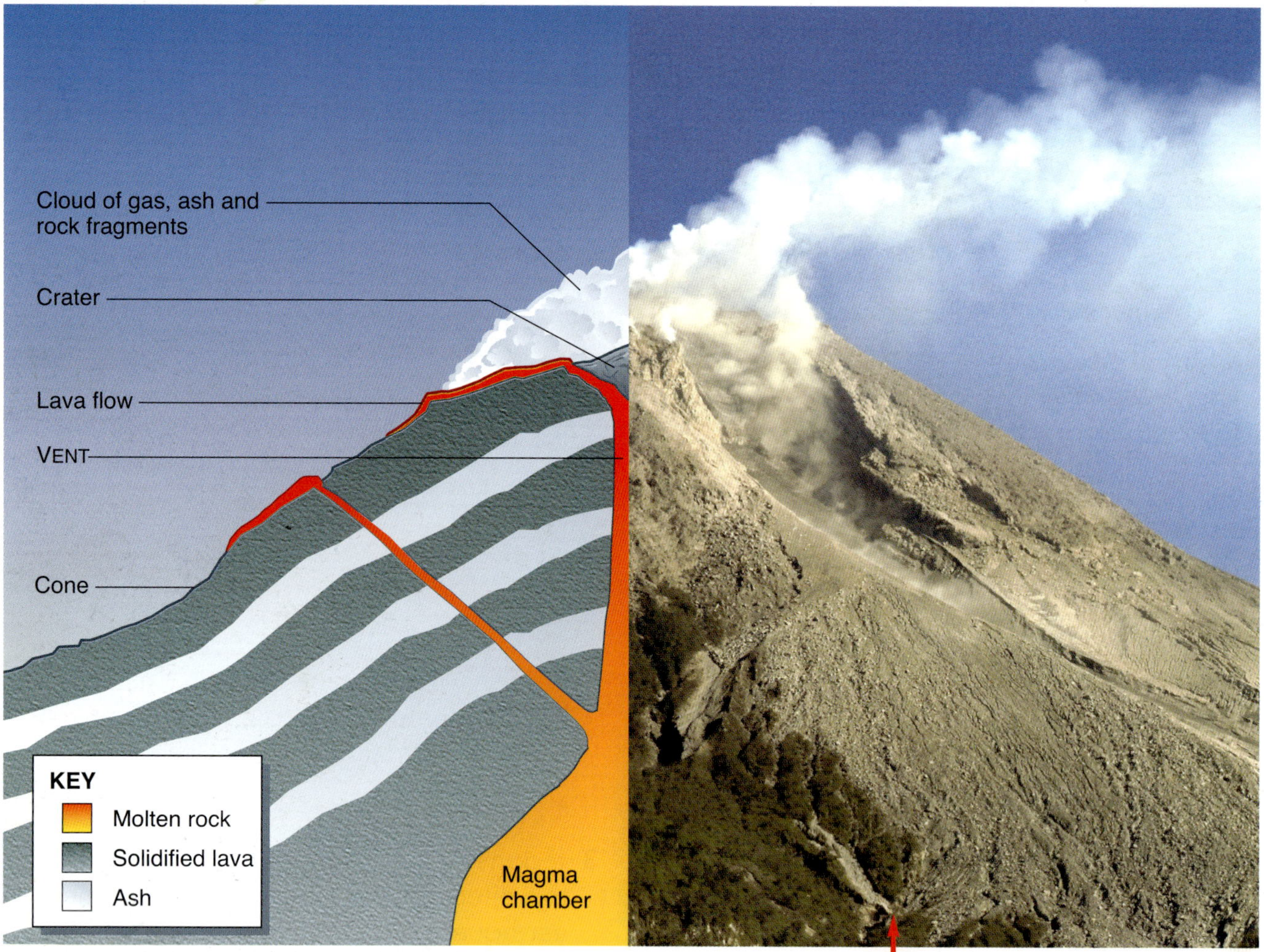

Merapi is Indonesia's most ACTIVE volcano. It has erupted 68 times since 1548. A major eruption happened in 1994. A dome of solidified lava at the summit collapsed sending PYROCLASTIC FLOWS (torrents of hot ash and rock) down the side of the volcano. Forty-three people were killed and thousands had to be EVACUATED from villages.

When Merapi is not active it is said to be DORMANT, or sleeping. A volcano that stops erupting altogether is EXTINCT.

WHAT MAKES INDONESIA SUCH A DANGEROUS PLACE TO LIVE?

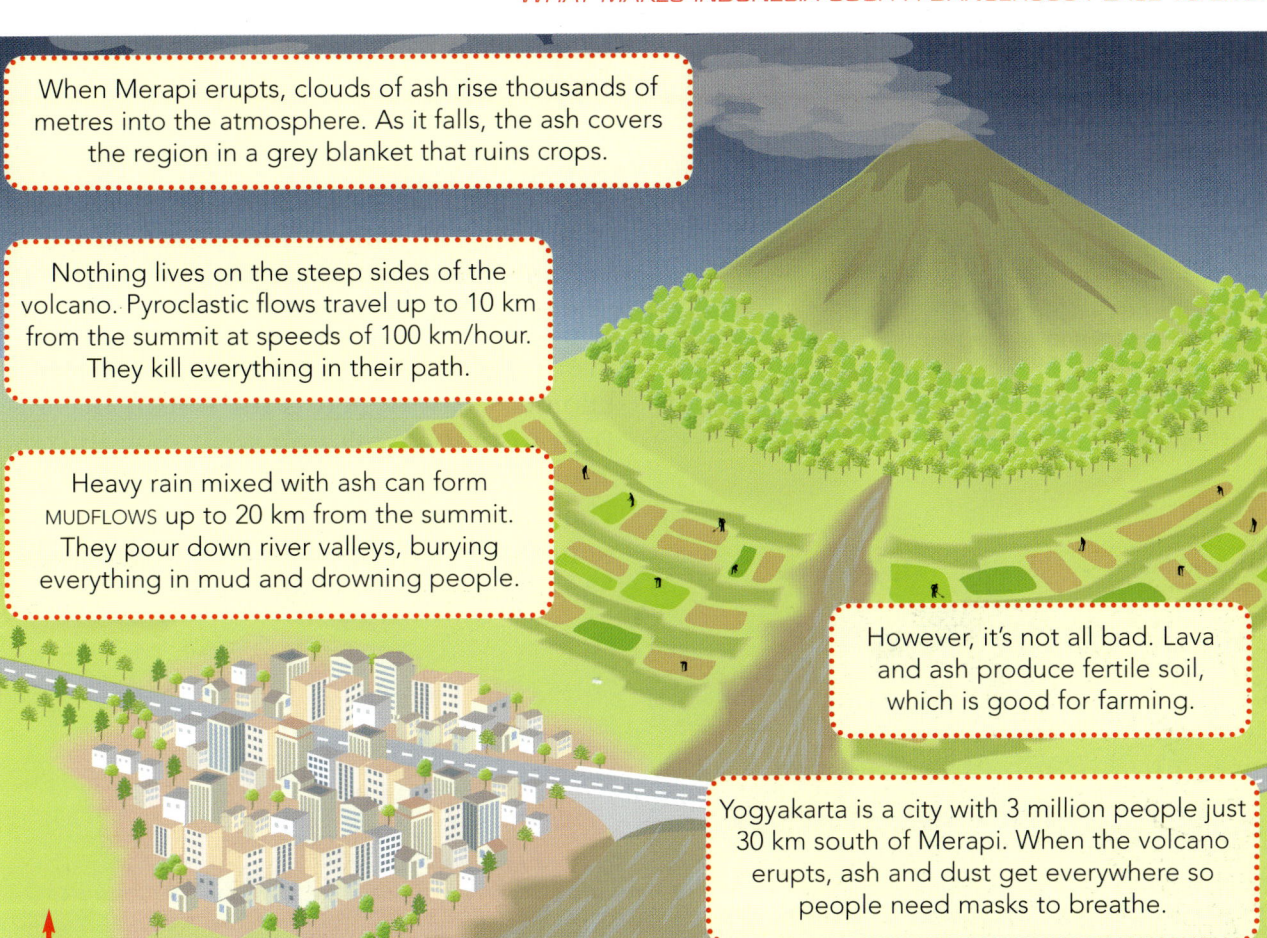

When Merapi erupts, clouds of ash rise thousands of metres into the atmosphere. As it falls, the ash covers the region in a grey blanket that ruins crops.

Nothing lives on the steep sides of the volcano. Pyroclastic flows travel up to 10 km from the summit at speeds of 100 km/hour. They kill everything in their path.

Heavy rain mixed with ash can form MUDFLOWS up to 20 km from the summit. They pour down river valleys, burying everything in mud and drowning people.

However, it's not all bad. Lava and ash produce fertile soil, which is good for farming.

Yogyakarta is a city with 3 million people just 30 km south of Merapi. When the volcano erupts, ash and dust get everywhere so people need masks to breathe.

S Impact of Merapi on Java

activity...

1 Look carefully at cross-section **R**.
   a) Match each label with the correct description below. Write them down.

   ★ molten rock from the volcano
   ★ pipe that brings magma to the surface
   ★ store of molten rock below the ground
   ★ circular opening at the top of the volcano
   ★ shape of volcano formed from layers of ash and lava

   b) Now, close the book. Draw a labelled cross-section of the volcano from memory. Use the descriptions you have written to help you.

2 Study the information in drawing **S**.
   a) Which dangers should each of these people be worried about? In each case give a reason.
      – a scientist climbing the volcano to study its behaviour
      – a farmer living 15 km from the summit
      – a resident of Yogyakarta
      – an airline pilot flying over Java
   b) If you were a farmer, would you continue to live near Merapi, or move away? Give your reasons.

aim high...

3 Go to the Volcano World website at http://volcano.und.edu
   Find out if Merapi is erupting now or, if not, when the most recent eruption was. Describe what happened.

LIVING ON THE EDGE

→ A blast from the past

A history of Krakatau

Krakatau was an enormous volcanic island in the sea between Sumatra and Java. It erupted about 60,000 years ago.

The eruption destroyed the island.

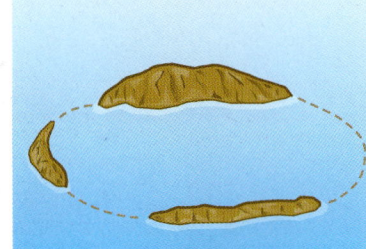

Slowly, over thousands of years, the volcano grew again.

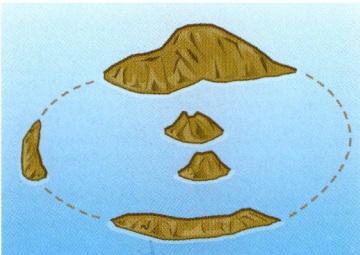

The volcano was destroyed again in the eruption of 1883.

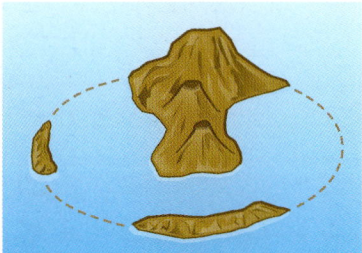

But, still Krakatau wasn't finished...

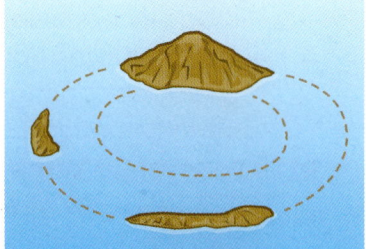

In 1927, Anak Krakatau (Child of Krakatau) appeared. It has been growing ever since. No one lives on the island.

At two minutes past ten on the morning of Monday 27 August 1883, Krakatau, a volcanic island in Indonesia, blew itself apart.

It was the world's most devastating eruption ever recorded. The sound was heard 5000 kilometres away, across the Indian Ocean. Dust from the explosion went high into the atmosphere and travelled around the world. That year, temperatures worldwide were reduced by 1°C. In Indonesia, more than 36,000 people were killed.

The events of 26 to 27 August 1883

1p.m. Sunday 26 August
The first explosions on Krakatau were heard. Billows of ash rose in the air and went tumbling down the mountain into the sea. An enormous cloud of dust from the volcano blocked the sun and the sky became dark.

8p.m.
Hot ash and rocks began to fall on the mainland of Sumatra and Java, up to 20 km away. People fled their homes afraid that their (thatch) roofs would catch fire. They had to protect themselves from falling rocks.

12p.m.
The explosions grew louder. They could be heard 900 km away in Singapore. In Jakarta, 140 km away, windows were shattered by the explosions.

WHAT MAKES INDONESIA SUCH A DANGEROUS PLACE TO LIVE?

T The volcano, Anak Krakatau, today

5:30 a.m. Monday 27 August
The first of four gigantic explosions came. The coastal towns of Ketimbang (in Sumatra) and Anjer (in Java) were destroyed by the tsunami wave that followed the explosion.

6:44 a.m.
The second explosion came. The ash cloud was so dense that the sun did not rise in Java. Ash began to fall in Jakarta. The next explosion at 8.20 a.m. cracked buildings in the city.

10:02 a.m.
The final, and biggest, explosion. A cloud of gas, ash and white-hot rock was hurled 40 km into the sky. The island of Krakatau was obliterated from the map. A tsunami wave over 40 metres high destroyed towns and villages along the coast of Sumatra and Java. Most of the 36,000 people who died were drowned by the wave.

activity...

1 Look at photo **T**.
   a) Draw a labelled sketch of the volcano. Label the following features:
      crater   *volcanic cone*
   b) Study the history of Krakatau. What do you think Anak Krakatau might look like in another thousand years? Draw another sketch from your imagination.

aim high...

2 Compare the events of 26 to 27 August 1883 with the tsunami on 26 December 2004.
   a) What similarities are there between the two events? Think of three.
   b) What are the differences? Think of three more.
   c) Could any lessons have been learnt from 1883 to prevent the disaster in 2004?

investigate...

Make more notes to help you to write your article. Look back at the last four pages (20–23) to make your notes. You have to investigate the question: 'What makes Indonesia such a dangerous place to live?'

LIVING ON THE EDGE

→ Front page news

Britain is a fairly safe place to live – much safer than Indonesia, for example. All our volcanoes are extinct. Occasionally we get a minor earthquake (if you've studied this unit carefully you'll know why). One of these earthquakes happened in 2008.

28th February 2008

AFTER THE EARTHQUAKE WE ASK – IS IT SAFE TO LIVE IN BRITAIN?

Re-read your article to check you answer the question

What happened?

Large parts of the country shook yesterday as an earthquake, six miles below the ground in Lincolnshire set off tremors that were felt around the country, from London to the Lake District.

The earthquake, the largest to hit Britain for 24 years, measured 5.2 on the Richter Scale and sent out tremors that spread 300 kilometres in all directions.

Chimneys toppled, windows cracked, pictures fell off walls, and close to the epicentre, a stone cross fell from the church spire in Market Rasen. There was one serious casualty. Student, David Bates, broke his pelvis as a chimneystack fell into his room in Barnsley, Yorkshire. Across the country hundreds of people dialled 999 to find out why their houses were shaking. Some worried people walked to the local police station in their pyjamas.

I like the way you use key facts

Fascinating information, but does it answer your question?

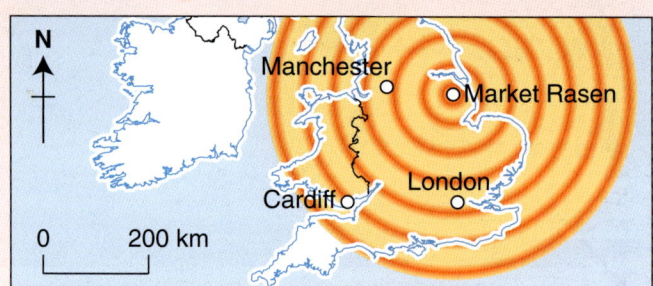

Where the quake was felt

This is a helpful map

Why did the earthquake happen?

Britain is hit on average by more than 300 earthquakes a year. Only about 20 of these are felt at all and it's only once every 20 years that we get one as strong as 5.2.

Britain is a long way from an active plate boundary, so earthquakes are quite rare. The tremors in Britain happen because the Atlantic Ocean is widening at a rate of a few metres every year. The huge forces that are pushing Europe further from America are eventually felt at small faults in the rock under the British Isles.

You've already said something similar. Don't repeat

I think you need to explain 'plate boundary'. Your readers may not understand.

Important information – it helps to answer the question (a diagram might help).

Is Britain safe?

Risks in Britain are low, but earthquakes have claimed victims here in the past. In 1940, one person died of a heart attack and another fell down the stairs.

Fortunately, in Britain, even when disaster strikes, as it did in the recent floods, we can rely on the emergency services to help out. As a wealthy country, we have the money and technology to put things right. So, compared with many other countries, yes, Britain is safe.

You could say more about this. Why is money and technology important?

Damage caused by the earthquake

Nice photo. You don't tell us where it is

WHAT MAKES INDONESIA SUCH A DANGEROUS PLACE TO LIVE?

■ your final task...

The deadline for your front page article is almost here. You should have made lots of notes to help you. Now, it is time to write.

This is what to do:
1 Read the article on the opposite page. It is similar to the one you have been asked to write. You could model your article on this one. Notice the comments from the editor, to highlight good points and things that could be improved.
2 Before you write, plan your article. Draw a layout for the page to show what you will include. Here is one idea.

You might find that it won't all fit on one page. You have a choice: either cut your ideas down to one page, or use two pages (your editor won't want one and a half pages!).
3 Write your article, including any photos, maps or diagrams.
4 Swap a copy of your article with a partner. They are going to be your editor! Comment on each other's article in the same way that the editor does on page 24. Highlight the things that you like and suggest ways to improve it.
5 Finally, redraft your article using the comments from your editor. Now, it's ready to be printed.

2 Save the rainforest!
Why does it matter if the rainforest is destroyed?

KEY CONCEPT
- Environmental interaction + sustainable development
- Interdependence
- Space

TROPICAL RAINFOREST is a natural ECOSYSTEM – a community of plants and animals. Around the world it is being destroyed at an alarming rate.

- The tallest rainforest trees grow to 60 metres – as high as a 24-storey block of flats
- One rainforest plant – the rosy periwinkle – is used to treat leukaemia in children
- A typical 10 km² area contains 1500 kinds of flowering plants and 750 tree species
- Sloths move so slowly in the trees that algae grows in their fur
- The forest has many dangerous creatures. The most deadly is probably the anaconda, a snake that grows to nine metres and can eat children

starter...

1 Talk with a partner. Discuss all your ideas about tropical rainforest.
Where does it grow? What is it like? Why is it like this? How is it changing? Who does this affect?
Now, write all your ideas down. Keep them until the end of the unit. At the end of the unit you will look back at your ideas. Some could be wrong and others may have changed. This will help you to select the information you will put into your rainforest guide.

WHY DOES IT MATTER IF THE RAINFOREST IS DESTROYED?

coming up...
There is something unusual about this rainforest. It is growing indoors!
This is the Eden Project in Cornwall. It is a celebration of the amazing diversity of plants on our planet – and, nowhere is more diverse than a tropical rainforest.

through the unit...
You will find out what rainforest is like, how people live there and why it is being destroyed.

your final task...
At the end you will produce a guide that will help visitors to the Eden Project to understand why the rainforest is so important, both for people living there and for us.

> The largest flower in the world grows here. It measures one metre across and it stinks of rotting meat!

> Rainforest is so dense that it can take ten minutes for rain falling on the trees to reach the ground

> One tree can house 200 types of insects – that's 200 types, not 200 insects!

> Rainforests cover only five per cent of the Earth's surface, but over half the world's species live there

2 Read the fantastic facts about rainforest on the photo. Take a minute to try to remember them. Then close the book.
   a) With your partner, see how many facts you can remember.
   b) Which do you think are the most impressive facts? (It's likely to be the ones you remembered.) Write them down. You could use them later in your rainforest guide.

discuss...

3 Look at the photo on the right, taken somewhere in the rainforest. With your partner, discuss:
   a) What is happening?
   b) What has it got to do with us?
   c) How do you feel about this?

Rainforest – an important ecosystem or just a load of trees?

Each year about 150,000 km² of tropical rainforest is destroyed – an area the size of England and Wales. Most of it is chopped down for timber, or to make space for farming. But, why should this matter to us?

SAVE THE RAINFOREST!

→ Ecosystems everywhere

The world is divided into BIOMES – huge ecosystems that cover the Earth's surface. Tropical rainforest is a biome. Map **A** shows you three more biomes: desert, deciduous forest and tundra. The natural VEGETATION that grows in each biome depends on the climate.

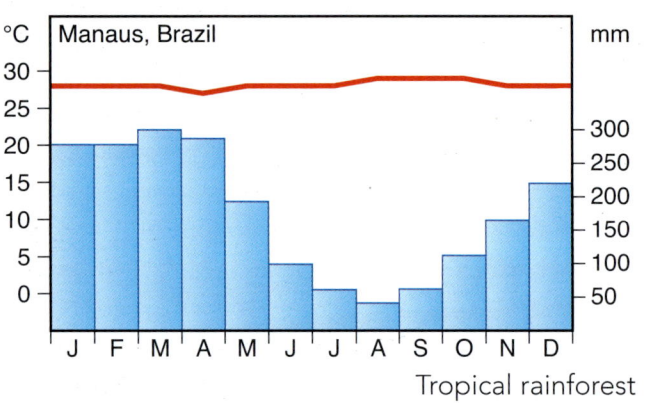
Tropical rainforest

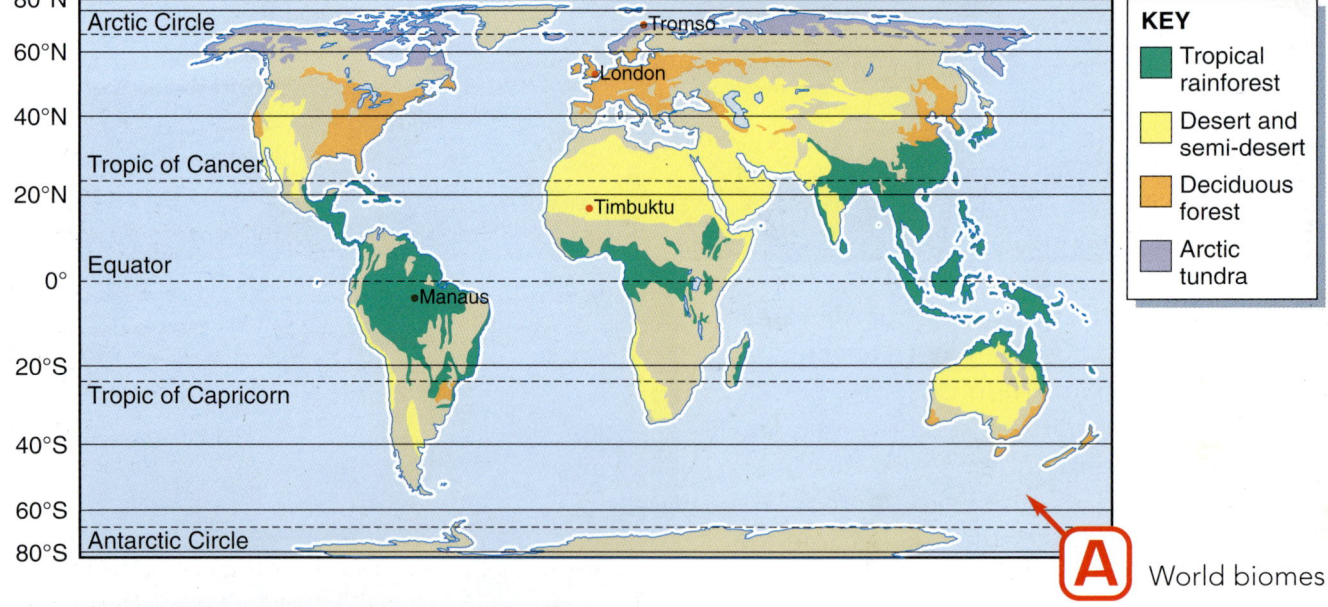
A World biomes

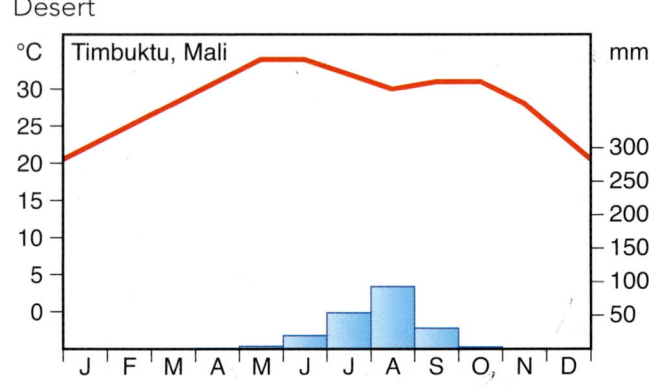
Desert

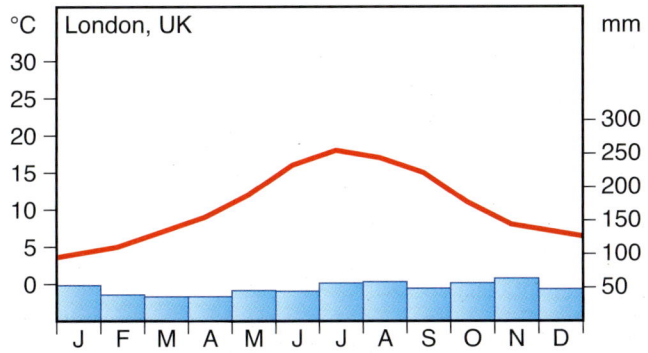

Deciduous forest (deciduous trees lose their leaves in winter)

Tundra

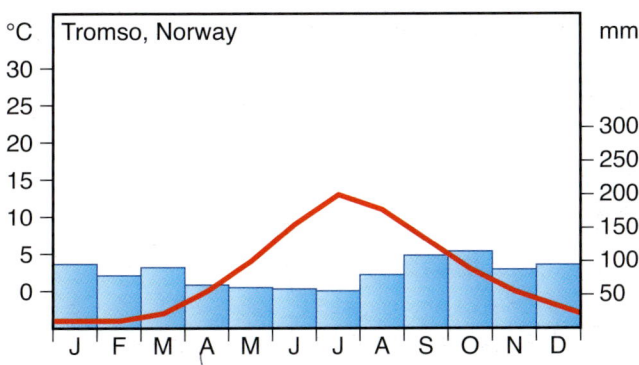

WHY DOES IT MATTER IF THE RAINFOREST IS DESTROYED?

activity...

1. Work with a partner. You will take turns to use the book.
   a) Choose one of the biomes on map **A**. Describe the distribution of the biome on the map to your partner without showing it to them. They shade the area you describe onto a blank world map. In your description, mention:
      - which hemisphere (north or south of the Equator)?
      - between what latitudes?
      - which continents?
      - coastal or inland?
      - to the east or west?
   b) Now, swap roles. Your partner chooses a biome and describes the distribution to you. Carry on until you have both completed the map. Together, when you have finished, compare the areas you have both shaded with map **A**. How could you have improved your descriptions?

2. Look carefully at the photos and graphs around map **A**. Complete a large table like this to describe: **a)** the vegetation, **b)** the climate, for each biome. One is done for you.

Biome	Vegetation	Climate
Tropical rainforest	Tall trees form a green canopy completely covering the land	Hot all year – over 25 °C. Wet most of the year, but less rain from June to October

aim high...

3. Most plants need warm, moist conditions to grow. Now, using this fact and the information in your table, answer these questions.
   a) Why do tropical rainforest trees grow so tall?
   b) Why does tropical rainforest stay green through the year?
   c) Which ecosystem has least vegetation? Explain why.
   d) What biome grows in Britain? Why is it suited to the climate here?

SAVE THE RAINFOREST!

→ It's a jungle out there

> A tangled mass of plants – trunks, boughs, leaves and reeds – rose up to tower above us as mysterious walls. The foliage came in a hundred different greens. Trees leaned over the river from both sides to drape their branches and creepers in the passing flow. It was as if the jungle was sagging at its edges, great waves of vegetation crashing down to engulf the progress of our boat, which now seemed small and fragile among the giant trees… But, through it, we just motored on, ploughing our lonely furrow deeper into the immense forest, as if we were travelling back to the beginning of time itself.

That's how explorer, Nick Middleton, described his journey into the tropical rainforest.

B Tropical rainforest

EVERGREEN TREES grow all year round in the hot, wet climate

EPIPHYTES grow on branches to be nearer the light. Their roots absorb moisture from the air

Ferns and shrubs enjoy the shade growing on the forest floor

BUTTRESS ROOTS stand above the ground to support the weight of the tallest trees

activity…

1. Read Nick Middleton's description.
   a) Identify the nouns, adjectives and verbs he uses to describe the forest. Underline a copy of the passage in three colours. Check any words you're not sure about in a dictionary.
   b) Now, use the words to draw a wordscape of the forest. First, draw an outline sketch of tropical rainforest. Then, write the words onto your sketch. Each word should form the object or shape they describe. For example…

Sagging

WHY DOES IT MATTER IF THE RAINFOREST IS DESTROYED?

EMERGENT TREES grow even taller than the rest to compete for sunlight

Trees form a thick **CANOPY** about 30m above the ground. They grow tall and straight to reach the light

Plants on the forest floor have large leaves to catch as much light as they can

LIANAS are plants that take the quickest route upwards by climbing tree trunks

Dense vegetation grows near rivers and in clearings where sunlight can penetrate

The soil is poor – trees have shallow roots to find nutrients near the surface

2 Plants ADAPT to the conditions around them.
  Look carefully at drawing **B**. How do the plants in a tropical rainforest adapt to the conditions?
  a) Describe at least five ways in which plants have adapted to the conditions, for example, *epiphytes grow on branches to be nearer the light*
  b) Design your own plant to live in the rainforest. It should be adapted to the conditions. Include as many of the features you mentioned in a) as you can.

aim high...
3 Identify five rainforest animals in drawing **B**. Write a sentence about each animal to suggest how they are adapted to life in the rainforest. For example, *a parrot can fly to reach the canopy where most of the fruits and nuts are found.*

31

SAVE THE RAINFOREST!

→ Living sustainably

Around the world about 50 million people live in tropical rainforest. Over thousands of years they have developed a SUSTAINABLE way of life that does little damage to the forest. Their knowledge of the forest provides them with all they need to live (photo **C**).

C An Amazonian Indian family living in the Brazilian rainforest

Food is obtained from the forest by hunting, gathering and fishing

Homes and boats are made using materials from the forest

Natural medicines, made from rainforest plants, can cure anything from headaches to heart disease

Plants provide for everyday needs including clothes, string, glue, oil and fuel

A small area of forest is cleared by chopping down trees and burning them

Seeds are sown in the clearing. The ash helps to make the soil FERTILE

The crops grow but, after two or three years, the soil loses its fertility

WHY DOES IT MATTER IF THE RAINFOREST IS DESTROYED?

Many products we use in our homes come from the rainforest. Compared with the average rainforest dweller, the way we obtain these products is much less sustainable. Often, it involves chopping down large areas of the forest.

E Rainforest products

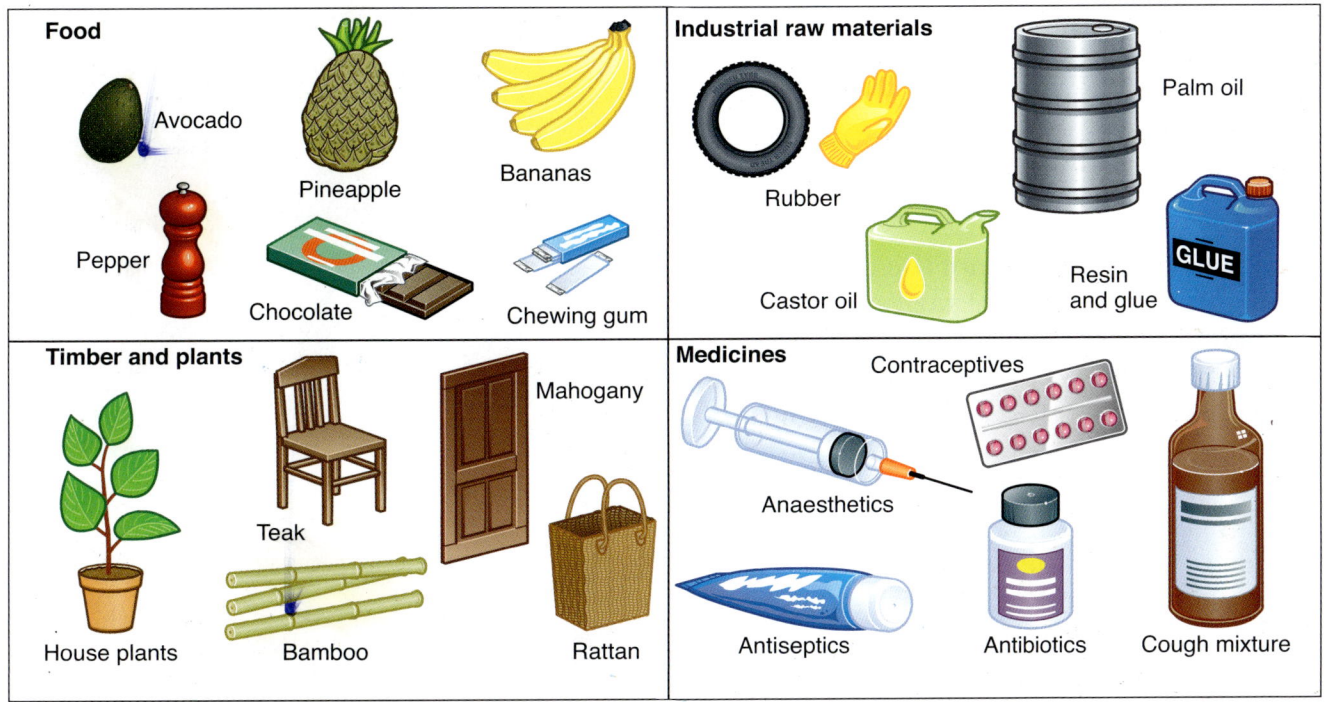

activity...

1. Look at photo **C**.
   a) List the ways in which rainforest inhabitants use the forest.
   b) Explain why this way of life is sustainable.

2. Look at the drawings in **D**.
   a) Complete a large diagram like this to describe shifting cultivation. Write four sentences in the spaces.
   b) Why do you think that this type of farming is sustainable?

aim high...

3. Look at the drawings in **E**. Choose one of the rainforest products and find out how we obtain it.
   - Where does it come from?
   - How is it produced?
   - How does this affect the forest?
   - Is this sustainable or not?

You can use a search engine like Google, on the internet, to do your research. For example, you can type 'mahogany' and 'rainforest' into the search engine.

D People in the rainforest practise a type of farming known as SHIFTING CULTIVATION

People move on to another part of the forest and the trees slowly grow back

33

SAVE THE RAINFOREST!

Whose forest is it?

The world's largest area of tropical rainforest is the Amazon region of South America, most of it is in Brazil. It covers an area almost the size of Europe. It is home to nearly a million Amazonian Indian people. Without the forest they would not be able to live.

Amazonian Indians are not the only group of people that depends on Brazil's rainforest. For poor people, living near Brazil's crowded coast, the rainforest provides them with land to build a new home and farm. For big companies, the forest is a never-ending source of valuable raw materials. And, for Brazil's government, it is a way of earning money to pay off the country's debts. As a result rainforest in Brazil is fast disappearing.

G An area of rainforest that has been cleared for cattle ranching

Brazil's disappearing rainforest H

F Amazon rainforest

Farming
Poor settlers clear the land by chopping and burning trees, then plant crops like rice or maize. Soon the land becomes infertile so they have to move further into the forest. The government has given plots of land to thousands of settlers.

WHY DOES IT MATTER IF THE RAINFOREST IS DESTROYED?

activity...

1 Study the information in drawing **H**. Which of these ways of using the rainforest is most destructive? Work with a partner.
   a) Write each of the rainforest uses on a separate card: small-scale farming mining   road building   cattle ranching logging
   b) Draw a line on a sheet of paper. Write 'Most destructive' at one end of the line, and 'Least destructive' at the other.
   c) Place the cards on the line, showing how destructive you think each one is.

2 If you were the President of Brazil, how would you decide to use the rainforest? Give reasons.

aim high...

3 Every time you eat a burger you could be using up a bit more rainforest. How? Design a simple information leaflet, for younger pupils in your school, to explain how eating burgers is connected with rainforest disappearing.

☐   ☐   ☐   ☐   ☐

← Least destructive   Most destructive →

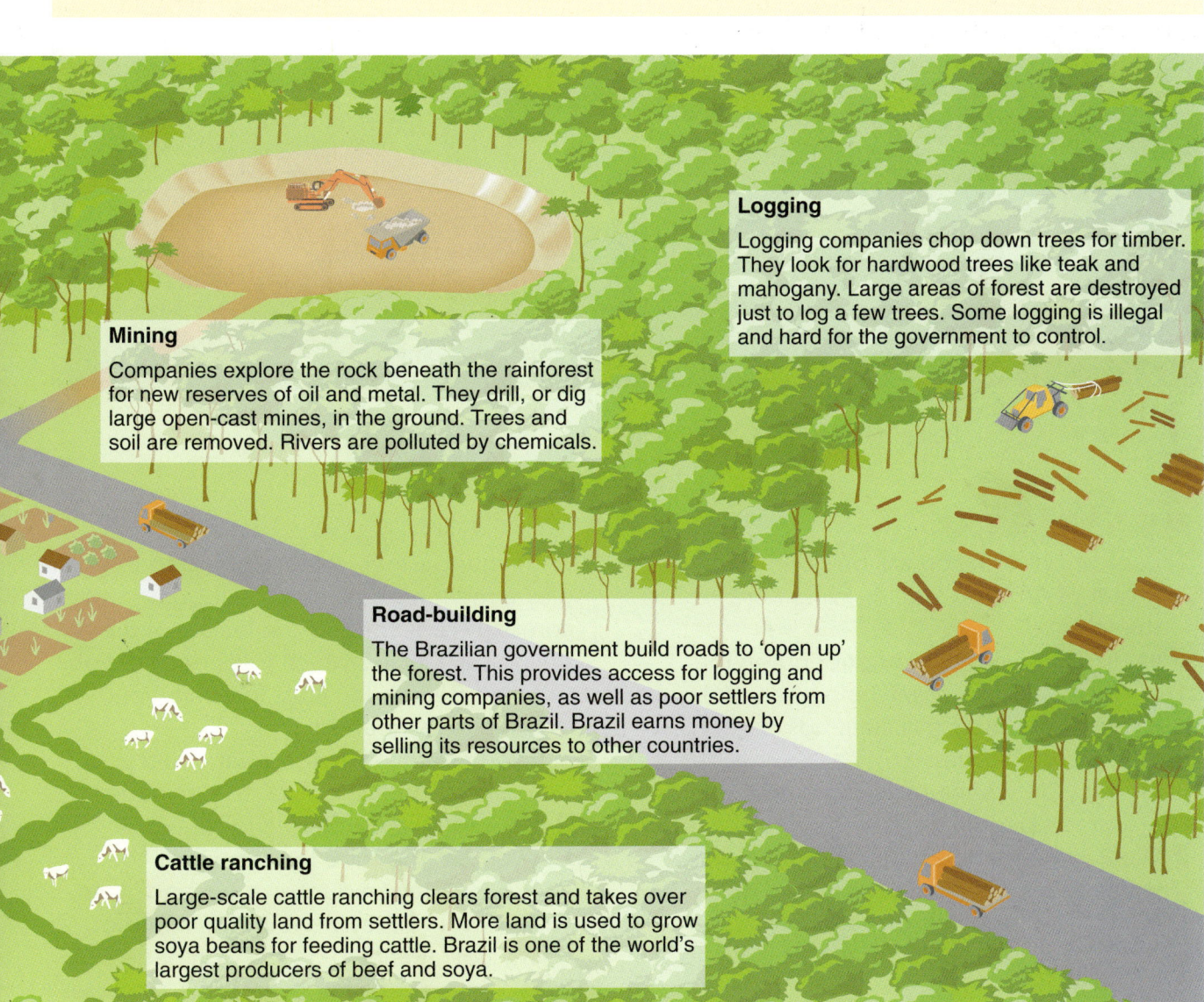

Mining
Companies explore the rock beneath the rainforest for new reserves of oil and metal. They drill, or dig large open-cast mines, in the ground. Trees and soil are removed. Rivers are polluted by chemicals.

Logging
Logging companies chop down trees for timber. They look for hardwood trees like teak and mahogany. Large areas of forest are destroyed just to log a few trees. Some logging is illegal and hard for the government to control.

Road-building
The Brazilian government build roads to 'open up' the forest. This provides access for logging and mining companies, as well as poor settlers from other parts of Brazil. Brazil earns money by selling its resources to other countries.

Cattle ranching
Large-scale cattle ranching clears forest and takes over poor quality land from settlers. More land is used to grow soya beans for feeding cattle. Brazil is one of the world's largest producers of beef and soya.

35

SAVE THE RAINFOREST!

→ Help! We need the forest

In Brazil the rate of DEFORESTATION is increasing. Each year, over 20,000 km² of forest is lost – an area the size of Wales. The Amazonian Indian people, who lived in the forest, are forced to move into towns and their traditional knowledge of the forest is lost.

> One day all this will be gone who knows what we will have lost?

> We do!

1 An isolated settlement in the Amazon rainforest

activity...

1 Look at photo I. You are one of the small group of Amazon Indians living here in the forest.
   a) In what ways do you depend on the forest? (Page 32 will help.)
   b) Why are the small clearings dotted around the forest?
   c) Why do you need so much space for so few people?
2 Work with a partner. A logging company wants to take over forest on the Awá's land to cut timber. It can offer jobs to some of the Awá people and a village in which to live. With your partner, you are going to role-play a meeting between the logging company director and the leader of the Awá tribe. Decide which roles each of you will play. Before you start, prepare your ideas for the meeting.
   - If you are the director, what could your company offer the Awá, to persuade them to give up their land?
   - If you are the tribe leader, would the Awá be prepared to give up land? If so, what would they want in return? If not, why not? (Read To'o's story on page 37.)
   Role-play your meeting. What is the outcome?

WHY DOES IT MATTER IF THE RAINFOREST IS DESTROYED?

The Awá are one of the last remaining tribes living in the Amazon rainforest in the Brazilian states of Pará and Maranhão. Over the past 30 years, much of the Awá's territory has been taken over by ranchers, loggers and settlers. Today, only 300 Awá remain, of whom about 60 still live uncontacted in small groups in the forest.

To'o, a member of the Awá tribe, tells his story.

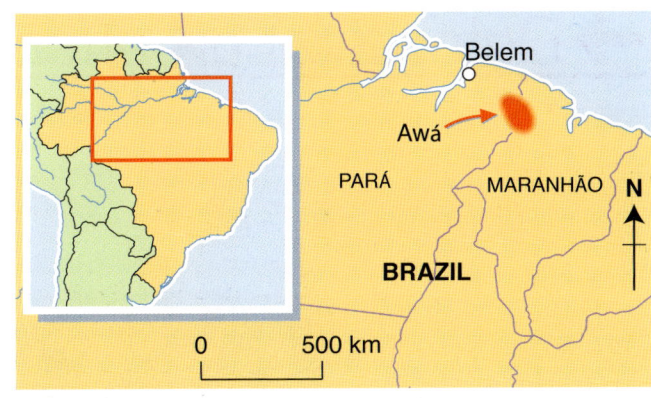

If the Indians have to leave their land, it will be very difficult. We can't live anywhere else because here there are forest fruits and wild animals. We couldn't survive without forest because we don't know how to live like white people who can survive in cities. We, the Indians, can't. The way the forest is being destroyed means it's much more difficult to find game (wild animals) because it's fleeing further and further away.

We have to preserve the forest or else we can't continue to live here. For years we've been fleeing up these rivers, with the whites chasing us, cutting down all our forest. We're going to fight for our land. We're not going to let the whites in. We're not going to let them finish our land. If we let them in, we'll soon be worse off than them. We want to raise our children here.

We love the forest because we were born here and we know how to live off the forest. We don't know about agriculture and commerce and we don't speak Portuguese (the main language in Brazil). We depend on the forest. Without the forest we'll be gone. We'll be extinct. The way things are going we will suffer from hunger and disease brought in by the whites. Every day as the population on our reserve increases so does disease like malaria and flu. We have to share the game with the settlers. They have guns so they kill more game than us. We are very worried about the lack of game and being able to feed our children in the future.

Source: Survival International

Survival is an international organisation with its head office in the UK. Survival helps tribal peoples defend their lives, protect their lands and determine their own futures. You can visit the Survival website at www.survival-international.org.uk to find out what is happening to the Awá now.

discuss...

3 Discuss these questions with a partner.
   a) The Awá want to keep their traditional way of life. What are the advantages of living in a forest rather than a city?
   b) Do you think the Awá should be allowed to have their own territory which no one else can enter? Why, or why not?

● SAVE THE RAINFOREST!

→ Deforestation affects us all

J Burning the Amazon forest

Deforestation happens all over the world – not only Brazil. Rainforest is being destroyed in many other tropical countries – from Cameroon to Costa Rica, Malaysia to Madagascar. In 1950, tropical rainforest covered sixteen per cent of the world's surface. Today, it covers just five per cent and the area is still shrinking.

activity...

1. Look at photo **J** and the two drawings.
   Explain to a poor settler in the rainforest why it is difficult to farm the land after they chop down the trees and burn them.
2. Look at the drawings in **K**.
   a) What impact could deforestation have on the environment at the:
      i) local ii) regional iii) global scales? Write a short paragraph about each.
   b) Which problem would be of most concern to:
      i) a rainforest Indian ii) a Brazilian city dweller iii) you?
      In each case give a reason.

discuss...

3. Discuss these questions with a partner.
   - What arguments would you use to persuade countries like Brazil that deforestation is not a good idea?
   - Do you think that Britain has any right to tell these countries that they should stop deforestation (after all, we chopped down our forests many years ago)?

K Effects of deforestation

SAVE THE RAINFOREST!

Another Eden

The Garden of Eden in the Bible was a symbol of paradise – a bit like a tropical rainforest, before people destroyed it! The Eden Project in Cornwall, like the original Garden of Eden, is a plant paradise.

The Project began in a giant, disused china clay pit that was completely lifeless (photo **L**). First, they built a huge plastic dome – they call it a biome – to create an indoor tropical climate. Then, they brought in the soil, the plants and, even, a few small animals to create something like a tropical rainforest ecosystem. However, there are no people living in this rainforest – just visitors.

The Eden Project under construction

L The Eden Project in Cornwall

- The tropical biome at Eden is the world's largest greenhouse.
- It is 240 metres long, 110 metres wide – bigger than four football pitches – and 50 metres high.
- Misters and waterfalls keep the air moist, and irrigation systems water the soil.
- The air temperature is kept between 18 °C and 35 °C.
- There are over 1000 plant species.

activity...

Look at photo **L** and the photo on pages 26–27.
1. In what ways is the biome similar to a real tropical rainforest? Think of at least three ways.
2. Now, think of at least three differences.
3. Do you think it would be easy to create a rainforest in Cornwall? Explain why.

WHY DOES IT MATTER IF THE RAINFOREST IS DESTROYED?

■ your final task...

You have to produce a rainforest guide for visitors to the Eden Project. The idea is to help them to understand why the rainforest is so important.

1. You are an expert on tropical rainforests now. But, how much did you know when you started this unit? Look back at what you wrote down in activities 1 to 3 on pages 26–27. This will help you to put yourself into the mind of a visitor to the Eden Project.
2. Plan your guide. You could divide it into three main ideas to explain why the rainforest is important.
   - It's unique
   - It's essential
   - It's irreplaceable (If you don't like these ideas, think of your own.)

Here are some of the key questions you could think about. You don't need to include them all – just the ones you think are interesting.

It's unique
- Where does it grow?
- Why does it grow there?
- What is it like?
- What plants and animals do you find?

It's essential
- How do people depend on it?
- How do people live there?
- How is it used?
- What do we obtain from it?

It's irreplaceable
- What happens after deforestation?
- How does this affect rainforest inhabitants?
- How does this affect us?
- How can the forest be used sustainably?

3. Produce your guide.
   Don't write too much – no more than a paragraph about each key question you include. Remember, visitors will be looking at the plants as they walk around. They won't have time to read lots of detail. Include photos, maps or diagrams to make your guide more visual.

3 India – a developing story

Which way should India develop now?

KEY CONCEPT
- Human processes
- Place
- Cultural understanding + diversity

coming up...

Prita is fourteen and is going to visit India with her family. It is almost ten years since she first went there. India is developing. Over ten years there have been some big changes. Now, Prita is going back to see the changes for herself.

through the unit...

You will travel with Prita to find out how India is developing and how it compares with other countries in the development league table.

your final task...

You will evaluate three different development strategies and decide which works best. You will recommend which way India should develop now.

WHICH WAY SHOULD INDIA DEVELOP NOW?

DEVELOPMENT means changes for the better. What signs of development can you see in India?

activity...

1. a) What is your image of India? Say what comes into your mind when you think of India. (Your teacher probably asked you to do this before you opened the book.)
   b) Which photo here is closest to your image of India?
   c) Do any of the other photos surprise you? Why?

discuss...

2. Study the photos carefully with a partner.
   a) What evidence of development can you see?
   b) Pick the photo that you think best represents development in India. Be prepared to explain why you chose this photo to the rest of the class.

INDIA – A DEVELOPING STORY

➜ Prita is going back to India

Prita is actually quite famous. This is not the first time she has appeared in a book. On her first visit to India (when she was five) her dad took lots of photos. Later, he turned them into a book called *Prita goes to India*. You can find it in children's bookshops and libraries.

This is Prita today. She has changed a bit in the past ten years!

Before I went to India I thought it was just a very big village with lots of mud huts and forests and cows. I guess I got those ideas from reading storybooks about India when I was little.

When I got there, it was completely different to how I imagined. There were lots of villages – thousands in fact. But, there were also cities. Huge cities crowded with millions of people. I just couldn't believe how big India was, and how many people there were. Indian cities are much more chaotic than cities in this country.

Even the villages weren't what I expected. My grandparents' house was in a village, but it wasn't a mud hut at all. It was a proper house with doors and windows, electricity and TV. Actually, it had most of the things that we've got at home.

I didn't realise how hot it would be. I knew that India was hot, but it was a completely different sort of heat. I went in the rainy season, so it was humid as well. As soon as I got off the plane I could feel my clothes sticking to me. Lots of people use air-conditioning in their homes. They need it!

I was surprised by the jobs people did. I thought they would all be farmers. But in my cousin's family they all did office jobs, like doctors or workers in the IT industry. Everyone seems to work hard in India, especially the women at home. Even the children worked hard. As well as going to school, my cousins had their own home tutors to help them to get good results.

WHICH WAY SHOULD INDIA DEVELOP NOW?

Prita is British. Her parents came to Britain in the 1960s. That was when migration from India to the UK was at its peak. India was less developed then, and there were fewer opportunities for work and education.

Britain's connections with India go back hundreds of years (find out more on page 56–57). Until 1947, when it gained independence, India was part of the British Empire. Even after independence, the links continued. Many Indians came to Britain for work, bringing their families here to settle. Today there are about one million people of Indian origin in the UK. Prita likes to think of herself as a British Indian.

Prita's family comes from the state of Orissa in eastern India. Now they live in London.

activity...

1 a) Find an old photo of yourself taken about ten years ago. Think about what you were like at that age. Describe at least five ways in which you have developed. Include things that you can't see. For example, *now you can read and write*.

  b) You can think of countries like people – they develop as time goes on. Think of at least five ways in which a country can develop. Again, you can include things that you can't see. For example, *better education*.

2 Look again at the photos on pages 42–43. You should find some examples of the connections between India and Britain.
  a) Write a caption for each photo to describe what you can see. For example, *8 A tea plantation*.
  b) Can you think of a connection with Britain? If so, explain the connection. For example, *In Britain we drink tea produced in India*.

3 Draw a large diagram, like this, using arrows to show the connections between India and Britain. One is done for you. You can include more ideas of your own.

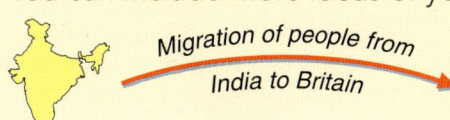

45

INDIA – A DEVELOPING STORY

→ India and the UK compared

One place in India that I've always wanted to visit is the Himalayas. Here I am with the Himalayas in the background. India is such a vast country and everything is on a grand scale. There are no mountains in Britain as big as this.

The map opposite gives you some idea of how big India is. Compare it with the UK shown at the same scale. Can you work out where Prita was when the photo was taken?

activity...

1. Look at this table. Use the data to compare India and the UK.
   a) Complete the sentence below to compare the area of India and the UK.
      India is about _____ times _____ than the UK.
   b) Now, write three more sentences of your own to compare population, life expectancy and urban population in India and the UK. Try to make your comparison as accurate as possible.
2. Compare population density in India and the UK.
   a) First, using data in the table, work out the population density for each country using this equation:
      $$\text{population density (people per km}^2\text{)} = \frac{\text{population}}{\text{area}}$$
   b) Write an extra sentence to compare population density for India and the UK.

aim high...

3. Does the data in the table indicate anything about the levels of development in India and the UK?
   a) Choose one indicator that you think tells you most about the level of development. Explain why you chose it rather than the other indicators.
   b) From this indicator, which country do you think is more developed? Explain why.

	India	UK
Area	3,287,000 km²	245,000 km²
Population	1,150 million	61 million
Life expectancy (average age of death)	63	78
Urban population (% living in cities)	28%	89%

WHICH WAY SHOULD INDIA DEVELOP NOW?

INDIA – A DEVELOPING STORY

➡ One billion people and rising

It's impossible to be alone in India. Everywhere I go there are people. Cities are the most crowded places of all, but even my grandparents' village is bigger than I remember. People in India have smaller families than they used to – especially in cities where women have careers. My aunt and uncle only have two children.

India's population reached one billion in 1999. That's one thousand million (or 1,000,000,000)! The graph shows that India's population is still growing. One day it is likely to overtake China, as the world's most populated country.

The rate at which India's population grows is slowing down. That's because its POPULATION STRUCTURE is changing (the proportion of people in each age group). More people are living into old age and parents are having fewer children. These are signs of development. You can see them if you look at how the shape of India's population pyramid is changing in **C**.

 Population change, 1950 to 2050 (India, China and UK)

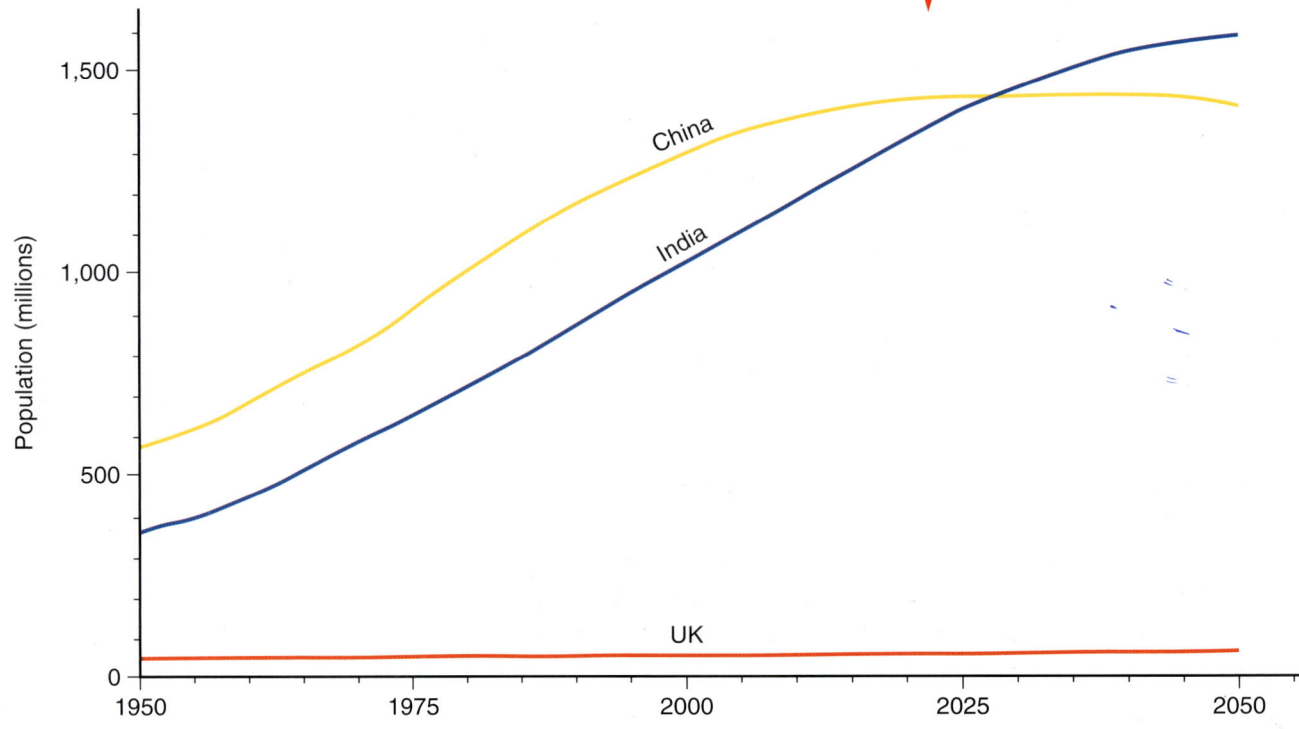

WHICH WAY SHOULD INDIA DEVELOP NOW?

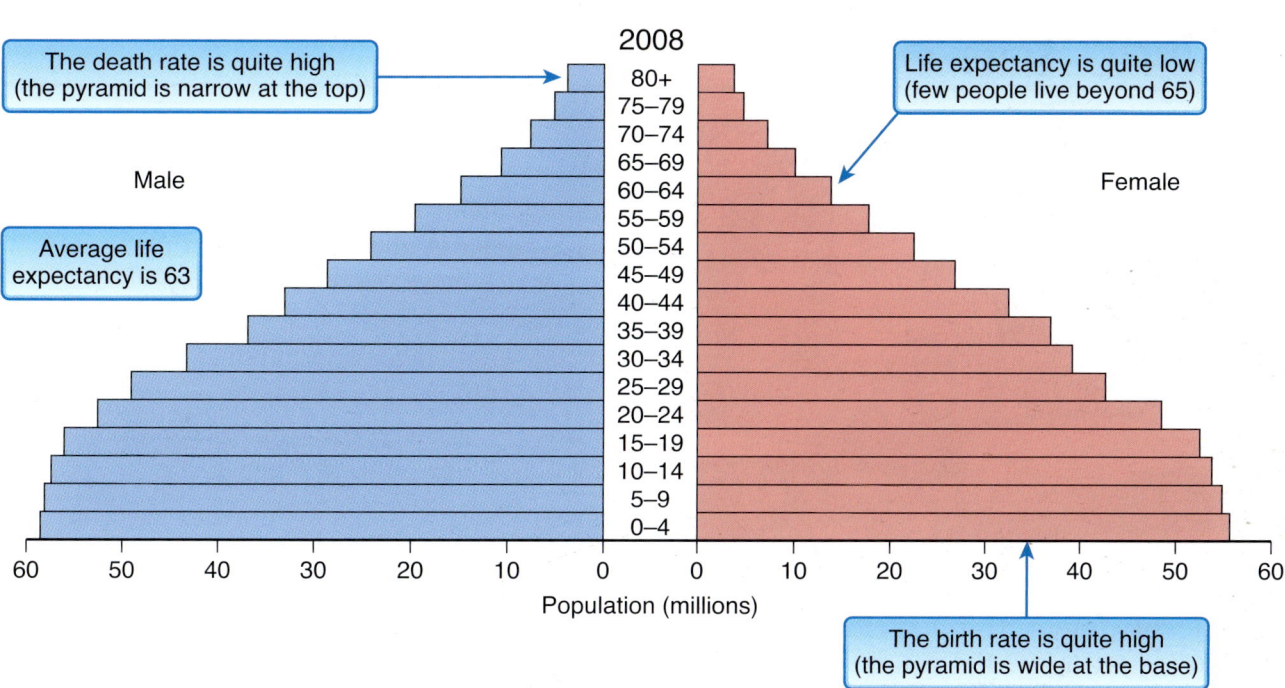

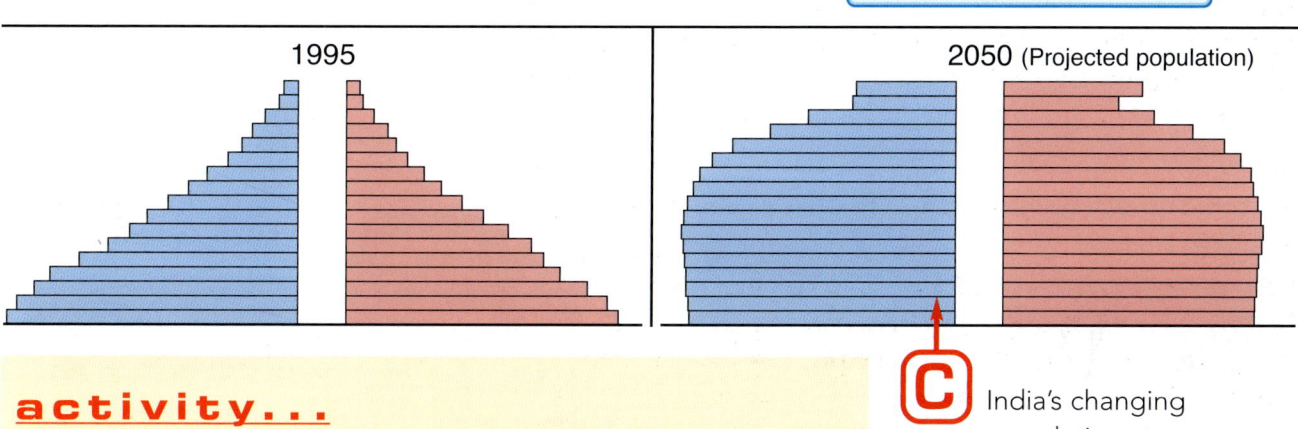

C India's changing population structure

activity...

1 Look at graph **B**. Answer these questions.
   a) What was India's population in 1950?
   b) What is its population now?
   c) What will the population be in 2050?
   d) When will India's population overtake China's?
   e) What happens to India's population after that?
2 Look at the population pyramids in **C**.
   Compare the pyramids for 1995, 2008 and 2050. Write three sentences to describe the changes in the proportion of people in these age groups between 1995 to 2050:
   a) under 15   b) 15 to 65 years   c) over 65 years.

aim high...

3 Study the pyramids more carefully. Read the labels on the pyramid for 2008.
   a) Look at the pyramids for 1995 and 2050. Describe the changes in life expectancy, birth rate, and death rate.
   b) Why do you think each of these changes is a sign of development?

49

INDIA – A DEVELOPING STORY

→ Mind the gap

No – this isn't my home in London. This is my cousin's apartment in Bhubaneshwar, a city in Orissa. His family is quite well off. Looking around the city I notice more wealth than ten years ago: shopping malls, people using mobile phones and wearing clothes with designer labels. I don't wear any of that stuff! But, there's a lot of poverty around too. I'm sure there are more beggars on the street now. They make me feel guilty.

There are now over 300 billionaires in India, more than we have in Britain. Wealth is a sign of development in India. However, INEQUALITY is growing, as the gap between the rich and poor is getting wider; 80 per cent of people in India live on less than a pound a day. In cities wealth and poverty exist side by side, like Mumbai in the photo below.

 High-rise apartments and a SLUM in Mumbai

Speech bubbles:
- The man from the city council says we'll have to move.
- Sanjay! Take the bucket to fetch some water.
- Why is our electricity bill so high this month?
- Don't forget your tutor comes tonight Swati.
- You've washed my school uniform Mum. What can I wear?
- The air is so polluted it's not safe to open the windows.

activity...

1 Look at photo **D**. You are going to make it a speaking photo.
   a) Read each of the bubbles around it. Where would you be most likely to hear each of them: in a rich family's apartment, or a poor family's slum dwelling? Think carefully!
   b) Your teacher will give you a copy of the photo and the speech bubbles. Stick the photo in the centre of a page in your book. Stick the speech bubbles around or on the photo, so that they come either from an apartment block or a slum dwelling.
   c) Make up two more comments of your own. Add them to the 'speaking photo'.

WHICH WAY SHOULD INDIA DEVELOP NOW?

E How to work out a country's wealth

GROSS DOMESTIC PRODUCT (GDP) is the total value of everything that a country produces each year. It measures a country's total wealth. It is the whole cake.

GDP PER CAPITA is what each person would get if GDP were shared out equally (but usually it's not!). It measures people's individual wealth. It is one slice of the cake.

Tales of wealth and poverty

The wealthy businessman
Mukesh Ambani is India's wealthiest man. Born the son of a petrol pump attendant, he went on to build his own business empire. His new home is a 27-floor skyscraper in Mumbai that cost more than a billion dollars (£500,000,000) to build. It enjoys panoramic views of the whole city. The first six floors are car parks, and the floors above that house hundreds of his staff. He and his family live on the top two floors, which also have a swimming pool and a helipad. Over the next few years, as other people become billionaires, more homes like this are likely to be built in Mumbai.

The poor farmer
Ravinder Kisan Piwar was a 23-year-old farmer in the region of Vidarbha in central India. He ran a small family farm, growing cotton to sell at the local market. The family relied on cotton to survive. But, in 2006, the price of cotton at market fell. That year Ravi earned less money from growing cotton than he spent on seeds and pesticides. The cotton he had grown lay in a pile going to waste and he couldn't afford to pay his debts. Eventually, it all became too much. He killed himself by swallowing a lethal dose of pesticide. Ravi was not alone. Over the past few years, 2000 cotton farmers in Vidarbha have committed suicide because they were in debt.

2 Look at cartoon **E**.
  a) Which country has the highest Gross Domestic Product: India or the UK?
  b) In which country are people richer: India or the UK?
  c) Explain the difference between your answers for a) and b).

aim high...

3 a) India's GDP/capita is growing quickly. Does this show that India is developing? Explain your answer. (Clue: remember, development means changes for the better.)
  b) Can you think of other ways to show that a country is developing? List your ideas.

- INDIA – A DEVELOPING STORY

→ There's more to development than money

Kunal's family is fairly well off as they have benefited from India's development. Many families in India are much poorer and have a different view of development.

This is my cousin Kunal. Apart from the fact he is a boy, we have quite a lot in common. We read a lot of the same books and we email each other to keep in touch. He is a year older than me and is planning to go to university. He wants to study science.

F

discuss...

1 Look at cartoon **F**. What is the message of the cartoon, do you think?

activity...

2 Work with a partner. Look at the aspects of development in **G**. Which aspects of development would need:
   a) money?   b) a change of law?
   c) a change of peoples' attitude?
   (Some may need more than one.)
   Draw a large diagram like this.

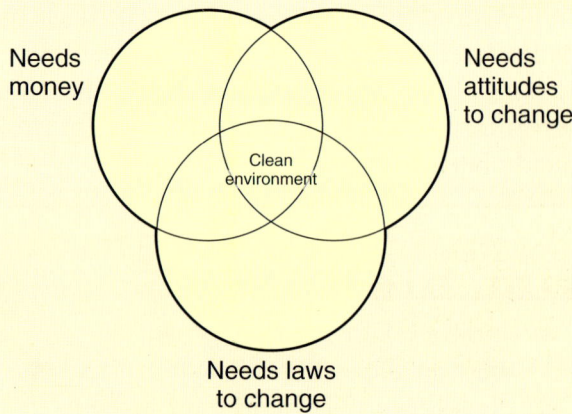

Write each aspect of development in one of the spaces in the diagram. For example, a clean environment might need all three.

3 Look again at the aspects of development in **G**.
   a) What would your priorities for development be if you were;
      i) a rich person in India?
      ii) a poor person in India?
      Mention three priorities for each person.
   b) Explain why their priorities are likely to be different.

aim high...

4 Now, think about the UK. What are your priorities for development in this country? Write a letter to the Prime Minister, giving reasons for your priorities.

WHICH WAY SHOULD INDIA DEVELOP NOW?

Good, basic, education

Enough food to eat

Clean environment

Justice for everyone — "Not guilty!"

Sharing wealth fairly — "One for you, one for me"

Clean drinking water

Living sustainably

Less Crime

Well-qualified workforce

Longer, healthier lives

Good energy supply

Wealth

Living in peace (without war)

Modern Consumer goods

Equal opportunities for men and women

Freedom to live without fear — "PROUD TO BE GAY!"

High quality health care

Reliable transport system

G Aspects of development

INDIA – A DEVELOPING STORY

→ India's position in the development league

> Kunal gets cross when I tell him that India is a less developed country. I think he takes it personally! Actually, I can see his point. It is a bit insulting to someone to call their country 'less developed' and your own country 'more developed'. It's not as if we've got everything sorted in Britain. I guess it depends on what you mean by 'developed'.

We compare levels of development in different countries using a range of DEVELOPMENT INDICATORS like the ones in table **H**. The countries at the top of the development league are MORE ECONOMICALLY DEVELOPED COUNTRIES, or MEDCs. The countries at the bottom are LESS ECONOMICALLY DEVELOPED COUNTRIES, or LEDCs.

activity...

1 Look at the development indicators in table **H**. Match each indicator with an aspect of development in source **G** on page 53. For example, *life expectancy* is an indicator of *longer, healthier lives*.

 Development indicators for five countries

Development indicator	Brazil	India	Kenya	UK	USA
Life expectancy (average number of years)	68	63	44	78	77
Adult literacy (% of adults who can read and write)	86.4	61.3	83.4	99.0	99.0
GDP per capita (US$)	7,450	2,650	1,010	26,580	36,110
Access to clean drinking water (% of population)	87	84	57	100	100
Infant mortality (number of children under 5 who die per 1,000)	34	70	76	6	7
Food consumption (calories per person per day)	2,974	2,496	1,976	3,276	3,699
Computer ownership (number per 100 people)	7.5	0.7	0.6	40.6	66.0
Inequality (% share of wealth for the richest 20%)	64	45	50	40	45
Enrolment at college or university (% of age group)	17	11	3	60	73
Environmental sustainability index (mark out of 100)	59.6	41.6	46.3	46.1	53.2

WHICH WAY SHOULD INDIA DEVELOP NOW?

2 You are going to make your own development league table for five countries: Brazil, India, Kenya, UK and USA.
   a) Choose the five most important indicators of development from table **H**. There is no correct choice. It is up to you.
   b) Write your indicators in the first column of a large copy of this table.

	Brazil	India	Kenya	UK	USA
Total score					

   c) Now look at the data in table **H**. Write a score for each country across each row in the table. Give a score of five to the country which does best for each indicator, four to the next best, and so on. For example, if you chose 'life expectancy' as one of your indicators you would write:

Life expectancy	3	2	1	5	4

   d) Work out a total score for each country. Which country appears to be most developed? Which country appears to be least developed?

aim high...

3 You are going to complete a world map to show HDI in different countries.
   a) Look at the data in table **I**. Divide the countries into four groups:
      - high HDI (over 90)
      - fairly high HDI (70 to 90)
      - fairly low HDI (50 to 70)
      - low HDI (below 50)
   b) Shade the countries on a world map using four shades of the same colour – the higher the HDI the darker the shade.
   c) Describe the pattern you see on your map.

It is difficult to say that one country is more or less developed than another country. To help, the United Nations (UN) uses three indicators to measure development. They combine the scores for GDP per capita, life expectancy and adult literacy to produce a HUMAN DEVELOPMENT INDEX (HDI) for each country. It is possible to score between 0 and 100. The higher the score, the higher the level of development (table **I**).

Human Development Index for some countries

Country	HDI
Australia	93.9
Brazil	77.7
China	72.1
Cuba	80.6
Egypt	64.8
Ethiopia	35.9
France	92.5
India	59.0
Indonesia	68.2
Japan	93.2
Kenya	48.9
Mali	33.7
Mexico	80.0
Nigeria	46.3
Norway	94.4
Pakistan	49.9
Peru	75.2
Russia	77.9
Saudi Arabia	76.9
South Africa	68.4
Spain	91.8
UK	93.0
USA	93.7

INDIA – A DEVELOPING STORY

→ How the development gap grew

Today, I'm wearing a silk sari. It is part of the traditional Indian culture I was brought up with. People sometimes think of India as a less developed country, but Indian culture goes back centuries. There was a time when India was just as developed as Britain.

India was not always less developed than Britain. The question is, how did India become 'less developed'? And, how did the world become divided between MEDCs and LEDCs? We can find out the answers by going back in history.

Long ago, India had its own civilisation. Some of the world's oldest cities and most stunning architecture were in India.

In the sixteenth century Europeans began to TRADE with India. There was a big demand for Indian textiles in Europe.

European countries fought with each other to control trade with India. Britain won. In 1600, they set up the East India Company.

The East India Company drained wealth from India. Cotton and other raw materials were sent back to Britain to supply the factories.

Meanwhile, the traditional textile industry in India could not compete with new, cheap cloth from factories in Britain. Soon they were buying textiles from us.

In 1858, the British government took control of India and it became part of the British Empire. The British united the country and built the first railway system.

WHICH WAY SHOULD INDIA DEVELOP NOW?

activity...

1 Draw a timeline like this across two pages in your book. The main events are shown on the line. Describe what happened before, between and since the main events.

aim high...

3 What might have happened if history had been different? Imagine that, in the sixteenth century, Indians had come to Britain to trade our wool… Write a story that ends with what the two countries might have been like today.

```
    East India                              British take      India gains
  Company set up                             over India       independence
────────┼────────────────┼────────────────┼────────┼─────────┼──────────
       1600             1700             1800              1900
```

2 Study all the information on this spread about the history of India and Britain.
  a) Draw a large table like this in your book.
  b) Complete the table by listing the ways in which the events in this story helped, or hindered, development in India and Britain. One is done for you.
  c) Who benefited most from the historical links between India and Britain, do you think? Explain your answer.

	India	Britain
Helped development	Indian cotton supplied factories in Britain	
Hindered development		

British rule did not improve life for most Indians. Thousands died in famines. It's no surprise that people began to call for the British to go.

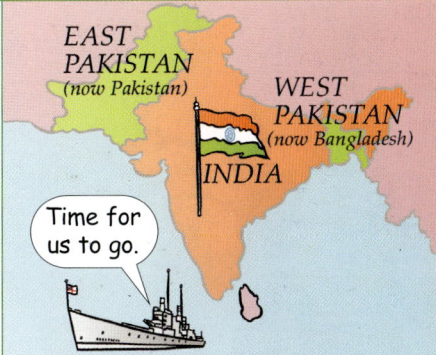

In 1947, India finally gained independence. The country was split into India (mainly Hindu) and East and West Pakistan (mainly Muslim).

The departure of the British caused chaos. Millions of Hindus and Muslims became refugees as they fled across the new borders. Many died in fighting.

Since 1947, many Indians, Bangladeshis and Pakistanis have migrated to Britain. They came because job opportunities and wages here were better.

Like other LEDCs, India borrowed money to develop. It invested in large-scale projects like roads and dams, as well as basics such as health and education.

The money had to be repaid. At the same time, the price of raw materials was falling (like cotton and tea). India got into a cycle of poverty and debt (like other LEDCs).

INDIA – A DEVELOPING STORY

→ Strategy 1: top-down development

Travelling to India with Prita you have seen how India has developed. Now we will visit three different development strategies.

TOP-DOWN DEVELOPMENT is a large-scale project (like a dam). It is initiated from the top, for example, by the government.

Building dams in the Narmada Valley

India suffers from widespread water shortage. Rain comes in one long deluge from June to October – the MONSOON. One solution to the problem is building DAMS. They allow huge volumes of water to be stored and used all year round. The largest water project of all is in the Narmada Valley in north-west India. It was initiated from the top, by the government, and aims to solve the region's water problems.

The Indian government says:

> Building dams means that farmers can IRRIGATE their crops all year round. That is vital if India is to feed its growing population.
>
> India does not have enough coal or oil to generate the electricity it needs. HYDRO-ELECTRICITY (HEP) is a cheap, renewable alternative.
>
> People in north-west India lack water. Women in rural areas can walk miles to collect water. Canals will bring water from the Narmada River to cities and villages.

The local protestors say:

> Over 300,000 people will lose their homes as villages are flooded. Farmland and forest will be lost too.
>
> Big projects don't help the poorest people. Half of India's children are malnourished and 40 per cent of homes still have no electricity, despite the dams that have already been built.
>
> It is estimated that the Narmada project will cost $8 billion over 40 years. There must be cheaper and more effective ways to provide everyone with water.

Protests against the Narmada Dam

WHICH WAY SHOULD INDIA DEVELOP NOW?

- The dam is used to generate hydro-electricity
- The reservoir behind the dam is 214 km long
- Water evaporates during the hot, dry season and is lost
- A new fishing industry is developing on the reservoir
- Farmland and villages in the valley were flooded by the reservoir
- The dam reduces the danger from flooding during the monsoon
- Water is used to irrigate farmland in the surrounding area
- Silt collects on the lake bottom and no longer fertilises farmland
- Water is sent by canal to cities in the region

J The Sardar Sarovar Dam, the largest dam on the Narmada River

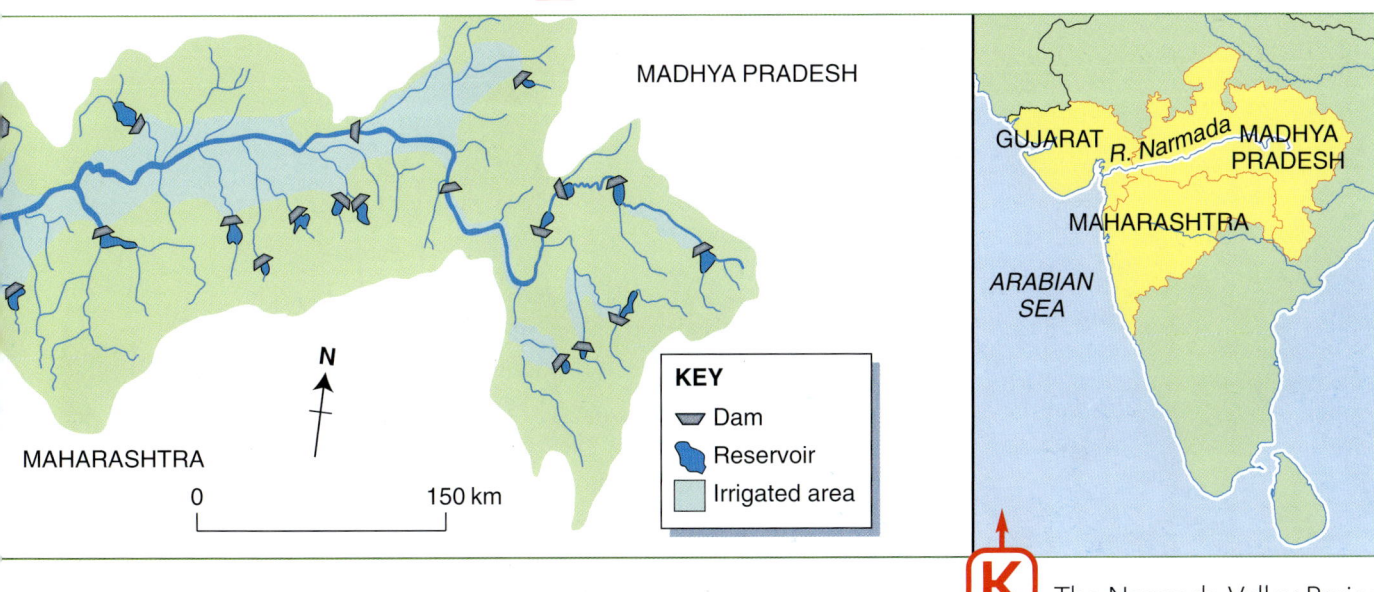

K The Narmada Valley Project

activity...

1. Make your own notes on 'top-down development'. Divide a page in your book in half. On one side note the advantages of the Narmada Valley Scheme. On the other side note the disadvantages.
At the end of the unit you will evaluate three different development strategies. You could work in a group of three to make notes and share them at the end. One person can make notes on 'bottom-up development' on pages 60–61 and another on 'outside-in development' on pages 62–63.

discuss...

2. Work with a partner. Role-play a meeting between a government official and a representative of the local community in the Narmada Valley to discuss the future of the region. Can you reach an agreement about what to do?

INDIA – A DEVELOPING STORY

→ Strategy 2: bottom-up development

BOTTOM-UP DEVELOPMENT starts with people rather than large-scale projects. It uses their skills and resources to meet the needs of local communities.

Education in Kerala

Despite its lack of wealth, India has a well-educated population. The state of Kerala in south India has the highest standards of education in the country. Nearly every child in Kerala goes to school. Education is the key to many other aspects of development.

	India	Kerala
Population	1,080,000,000	32,000,000
School attendance	79%	97%
Adult literacy	61%	91%
Life expectancy	63	73
Human Development Index	59	72.0

L A secondary school classroom in India

activity...

1 Look at photo **L**.
   a) Describe at least three differences between this classroom and yours.
   b) How would each of these differences affect the quality of education?

2 Look at the photos on page 61.
   a) How would education help each of these people to do their jobs?
   b) What contribution is each person making to India's development?

WHICH WAY SHOULD INDIA DEVELOP NOW?

Farmer

Film star

Engineer

IT worker

3 Make your own notes on 'bottom-up development'. Divide a page in your book in half. On one side note the advantages of Kerala's education. On the other side note the disadvantages.
4 Look at the scattergraph on the right. It compares school attendance and adult literacy in 16 states in India.
   a) Describe the pattern on the graph. How does adult literacy change as school attendance increases?
   b) How do you explain the connection between education and adult literacy?

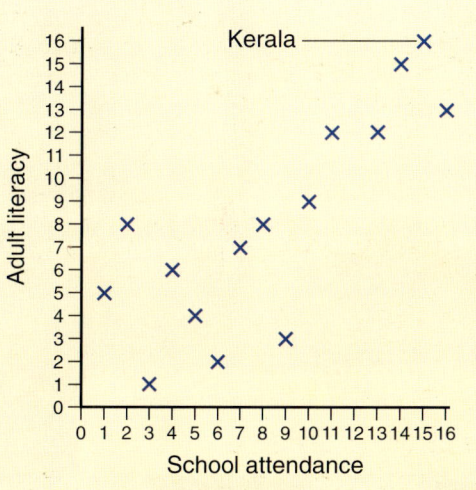

aim high...

5 Think about how education could affect other aspects of development such as GDP/capita or life expectancy. Do you think that education is really the key to development? Write a paragraph to explain your answer.

INDIA – A DEVELOPING STORY

→ Strategy 3: outside-in development

These days, when we phone a bank, book an air flight or enquire about a train timetable, we could be talking to someone in an Indian call centre. Many British and American companies now OUTSOURCE their activities to India. This means that jobs that were once done here are done there. It is part of the process of GLOBALISATION – the rapid spread of ideas and activities around the world. Outsourcing is an example of OUTSIDE-IN DEVELOPMENT.

Outsourcing in Hyderabad

Recent improvements in communications technology (like satellites and the internet) have made it possible for transnational companies to outsource activities from MEDCs to LEDCs. The driving force for this change is lower wages, but it is not just the companies who benefit. Indian workers can earn more money than they did before. The government also collects more in taxes from people's wages and company profits.

M Cyberabad (a suburb of Hyderabad) where many transnational companies are based

Modern, state-of-the-art buildings with 24-hour electricity and good communication links

The state government of Andra Pradesh offers subsidies to companies that create jobs

India has a well-educated workforce that speaks English

Indian workers are cheaper to employ than workers in MEDCs, like the UK

WHICH WAY SHOULD INDIA DEVELOP NOW?

Spare a thought for me. I spend every day (actually, it's night-time in India) dealing with lots of angry British customers on the telephone. Most of them want to cancel their accounts with our company. My job is to persuade them not to.

Before I started the job, I was trained in listening skills and telephone etiquette. I was given a crash course in British culture (from fish and chips to football teams) to help me to understand the people I talk to. For example, I was warned that the British public listen quietly on the phone. When there is silence an Indian person might panic, and think that the person on the end of the line is dead, or shout loudly to wake them up!

We work according to British time, five and a half hours behind Indian time. That means we work late into the night. There is a map of Britain on the wall so that I know where the customer is, and I listen to the British weather forecast so that I can talk to them about the weather.

Working in a call centre is like being a robot. We have to follow the same script with each customer. It's like being in another world. I sit looking at my computer screen for nine hours every day with a headset over my ears. All around me are hundreds of other workers sitting in long rows, behind identical desks, doing the same jobs as me.

Eventually I think the job will drive me mad. I already find myself talking to customers in my sleep. I get confused about who I am. Am I Indian or British? Is my name Alok or Alan (the name I tell my customers)? Many of my colleagues have left the job. I want to do the same, but what is the alternative? I could work for a local company on less than half the wages, or I could go back to my family village and no job at all.

A call centre worker

activity...

1 Look at photo **M**. Design an advert for Cyberabad to attract British-based companies to outsource their activities to India.
2 Read about Alok's experience working in an Indian call centre. Then, answer these questions:
   a) Why is it important that he knows about Britain?
   b) Why does he have to work at night?
   c) If the job is that bad, why does he do it?
   d) If you were speaking to Alok on the phone, what questions would you like to ask him? (Unfortunately, he couldn't answer you because he's got to stick to his script!)
3 Make your own notes on 'outside-in development'. Divide a page in your book in half. On one side, note the advantages of outsourcing in Hyderabad for India. On the other side, note the disadvantages for India.
4 a) Suggest why each of these people would think that globalisation is a good idea:
      i) Bill Gates, the owner of Microsoft
      ii) the prime minister of India
      iii) an Indian student.
   b) Can you think of anyone who would think that globalisation is a bad idea? Explain why.

aim high...

5 Are you for or against globalisation? Write a short speech that you could give in a debate. Your teacher might ask you to give the speech in a class debate.

INDIA – A DEVELOPING STORY

➡ Which is the way to develop?

The summer holiday is over. I'm back at school in my Geography lesson. India feels a million miles away. But, it's not really – it's just a phone call or an email away.

We're studying development this year. My teacher says development is about changes for the better. Not all the changes that I saw in India were for the better. There is more wealth and people live longer, but there is also more pollution and greater inequality. If development in India was up to me I would do more to help the poor.

There is more than one way for a country to develop. It all depends on what you think development is about. Here are some ideas.

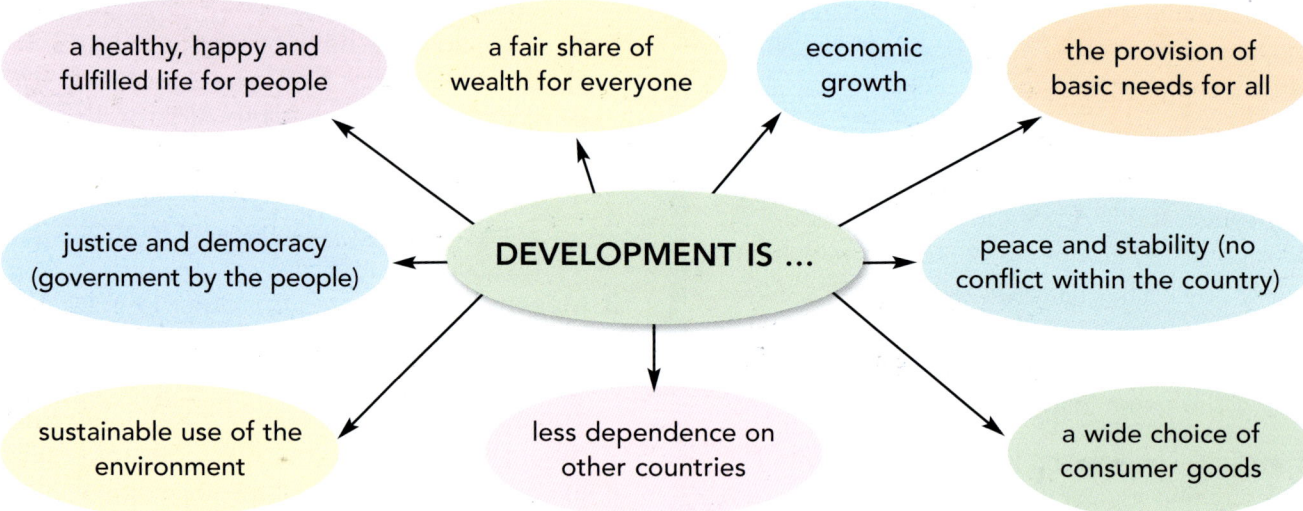

DEVELOPMENT IS ...
- a healthy, happy and fulfilled life for people
- a fair share of wealth for everyone
- economic growth
- the provision of basic needs for all
- justice and democracy (government by the people)
- peace and stability (no conflict within the country)
- sustainable use of the environment
- less dependence on other countries
- a wide choice of consumer goods

discuss...

Work with a partner. If you were in charge of a country, what would be your priorities for development? Rank the ideas above in order of importance.

Write the ideas onto cards. Then arrange them into a diamond rank formation like this.
Put your most important idea at the top, the next two most important ideas below, and so on.

```
        1
      2   2
    3   3   3
      4   4
        5
```

WHICH WAY SHOULD INDIA DEVELOP NOW?

your final task...

Through this unit you have travelled to India with Prita and seen how the country is developing. You have also seen different development strategies at work. You are now quite a development expert!

1 You are going to evaluate the three development strategies that you have seen in India. If you worked in a group of three, now is the time to share your notes.

Look back at the three development strategies:
- Top-down development – building dams in the Narmada Valley
- Bottom-up development – education in Kerala
- Outside-in development – outsourcing in Hyderabad

Evaluate each strategy using the priorities for development in your diamond. Which priorities does each strategy help to meet? You could draw copies of the diamond and tick the priorities each strategy meets.

2 As the development expert, you have to recommend how India should develop now. Write a short report for the Indian government. Write three paragraphs, to answer the following questions:
a) Which strategy do you most recommend, and why? You can refer to your evaluation.
b) How does this strategy work? Refer to an example that you have seen in India of this strategy working.
c) Do you recommend any other strategies? If so, which ones and why? If not, why not? Again, you can refer to examples you have seen in India.

Top-down development – building dams

Bottom-up development – education

Outside-in development – outsourcing

4 Food for the future

What are the ingredients for a better world?

KEY CONCEPT

- **Interdependence**
- Environmental interaction + sustainable development
- Scale

Our food comes from all over the world. The ingredients in this pizza have travelled thousands of kilometres to get here.

- The pizza base uses flour made from wheat grown in the USA
- Tomato sauce is made from tomatoes grown in Spain
- Mozzarella cheese is produced in Italy
- Pineapples are grown in Kenya
- Sweetcorn is grown in Canada
- Ham comes from pigs reared in Denmark
- Peppers are grown in the Netherlands

WHAT ARE THE INGREDIENTS FOR A BETTER WORLD?

coming up...

Everyone knows that it is important to eat healthy food because it is good for your body. However, did you know that what you eat can also be good for the rest of the world? What you eat can affect your health, but it can also affect whether a chicken lives a happy life, whether a poor farmer in Africa can afford to send his children to school, or it can even affect the future for our planet.

through the unit...

You start with a recipe for your favourite meal. Then you will find out more about where food comes from, who produces it, and how it is produced. As you do, you might decide to change some of your ingredients.

your final task...

You rewrite your recipe so that it is good for the rest of the world, as well as for you. By now, you might have quite a different meal – and, with luck, you'll get a chance to cook it!

starter...

1. We measure how far our food has travelled in FOOD MILES or FOOD KILOMETRES. Work out the food kilometres for this pizza.
   a) Where does each ingredient come from? Find each country on a map of the world (or use Google Earth).
   b) Roughly, work out the distance in kilometres from each country to the UK, using the scale on the map (or use the measuring tool on Google Earth). For example, Spain to the UK is 1300 km.
   c) Complete a table like this:

Ingredient	Country	Distance (km)
Tomatoes	Spain	1,300

   d) Add the distances together to find the total number of food kilometres that the pizza has travelled.

your recipe...

What is your favourite meal? Think of a two-course meal that you could cook, including a main course and a dessert.
1. Write a list of the ingredients for your meal. (If you're not sure of the ingredients, find a recipe in a cookbook or on the internet.)
2. Investigate all the ingredients at your local supermarket. Where do they come from? Make a list of the countries.
3. Work out the food kilometres for your meal, using the same method as the Starter.

This pizza has travelled further than you might think!

FOOD FOR THE FUTURE

→ Why food miles matter

If you go to a supermarket today, you will find foods from all over the world (**A**). Do you know where they come from? Do you even know what they are? Unless you look closely at the labels, you won't know whether they come from Britain or another country.

It wasn't always like this. Did you know that 50 years ago, most of the food in the shops was locally produced? Fresh food could only be bought in certain seasons (like strawberries in June). Some people think we should reconnect with the food we eat and go back to this type of shopping.

A Fresh foods in the supermarket. What are they? Where do they come from?

activity...

1 Look at the pictures of fruit and vegetables in **A**.
   a) What are the foods?
   b) Which ones are grown in Britain?
If you're not sure, turn the book upside down for the answers.
2 Read the statements about food miles in box **B**.
   a) Sort the statements into two groups
      i) benefits
      ii) problems of more food miles.
   b) For each of the four people, choose one statement they might think is most important.
   c) On balance, would each person be for or against more food miles? Why?
   d) Now, make your own decision. Are you for or against more food miles? Give some reasons.

your recipe...

Look again at your recipe. Where do the ingredients come from? How far have they travelled?

Having studied these two pages, do you want to change your food miles? Could you find the same ingredients somewhere else? Where do you want the ingredients to come from: Britain or abroad? For example, if you want to reduce your food miles you could decide to use British apples rather than New Zealand ones.

If necessary, rewrite your recipe.

Answers: 1 a) asparagus, kiwi fruit, butternut squash, mangetout, leeks, blueberries b) All of them! However, you will also find the same foods imported from other countries.

WHAT ARE THE INGREDIENTS FOR A BETTER WORLD?

African farmer

British shopper

a) Transporting food long distances means that planes and lorries burn more fuel and produce more carbon emissions, making global warming worse.

b) Many foods can now be brought all year round, not just when they are in season in Britain.

c) Fresh food loses its vitamin content during the time it takes to travel long distances.

d) Many of the foods that used to be grown in this country are no longer grown because they can be grown elsewhere.

e) Farmers in poor countries depend on selling export crops to earn money to help them and their families survive.

f) Certain crops grow better in a warm climate. They will only grow in Britain in a greenhouse.

g) The more lorries that carry food long distances, the more traffic congestion there is on the road.

h) If we rely on imported food it makes our food supply vulnerable, especially if there is an oil shortage or a transport problem.

i) Food that travels long distances needs more packaging to prevent it from being damaged.

j) It is difficult to regulate the standards of our food if it comes from other countries.

k) There is a wide variety of foods available in supermarkets from around the world, offering more choice.

l) Food produced in poor countries is often cheaper because of the low cost of labour.

m) The food varieties that travel best, and have the longest shelf life, don't always taste so good.

n) Most of the household waste in Britain comes from food packaging in supermarkets.

o) Exporting food to Europe is vital to the economy in many poor countries.

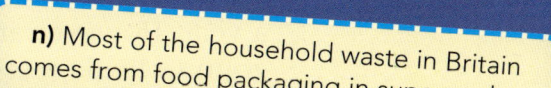
British farmer

 Food miles

Environmentalist

FOOD FOR THE FUTURE

→ Overweight – and over here!

Britain has a problem with obesity. A growing number of people are overweight, including children. Obesity is linked with health problems such as heart disease and diabetes.

Look at map **C**. The recommended daily intake of calories for a healthy diet is 2000 for women and 2500 for men. In Britain (and other rich countries) the average daily calorie intake is well above this figure. We have the problem of being overfed. In poor countries it is the opposite problem – many people are underfed. Eighteen million die each year from hunger or hunger-related diseases. So, you might be surprised that there is more than enough food in the world to feed everyone!

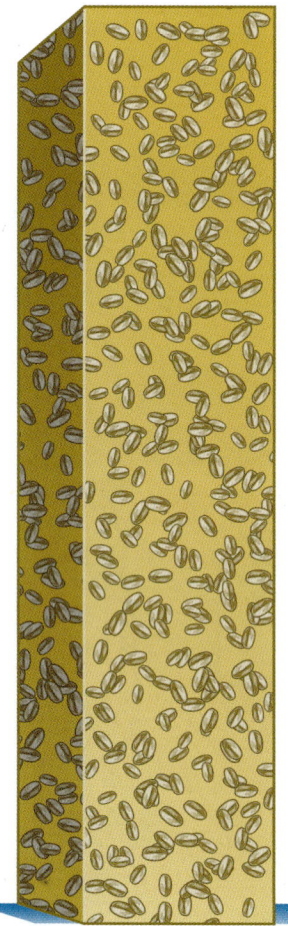
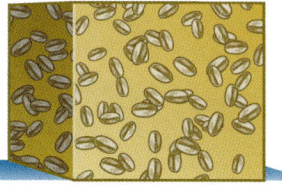

C Feeding the world

The problem is that much of the food we produce is used to feed animals rather than people. It takes just 180 kilograms of grain (wheat, barley, rice, etc) to feed a person for a year. However, it takes 930 kilograms of grain to feed a person eating meat (graph **D**). All the grain is used up feeding the animals (read more on pages 72–73).

 Grain consumption for people eating grain or meat (per year)

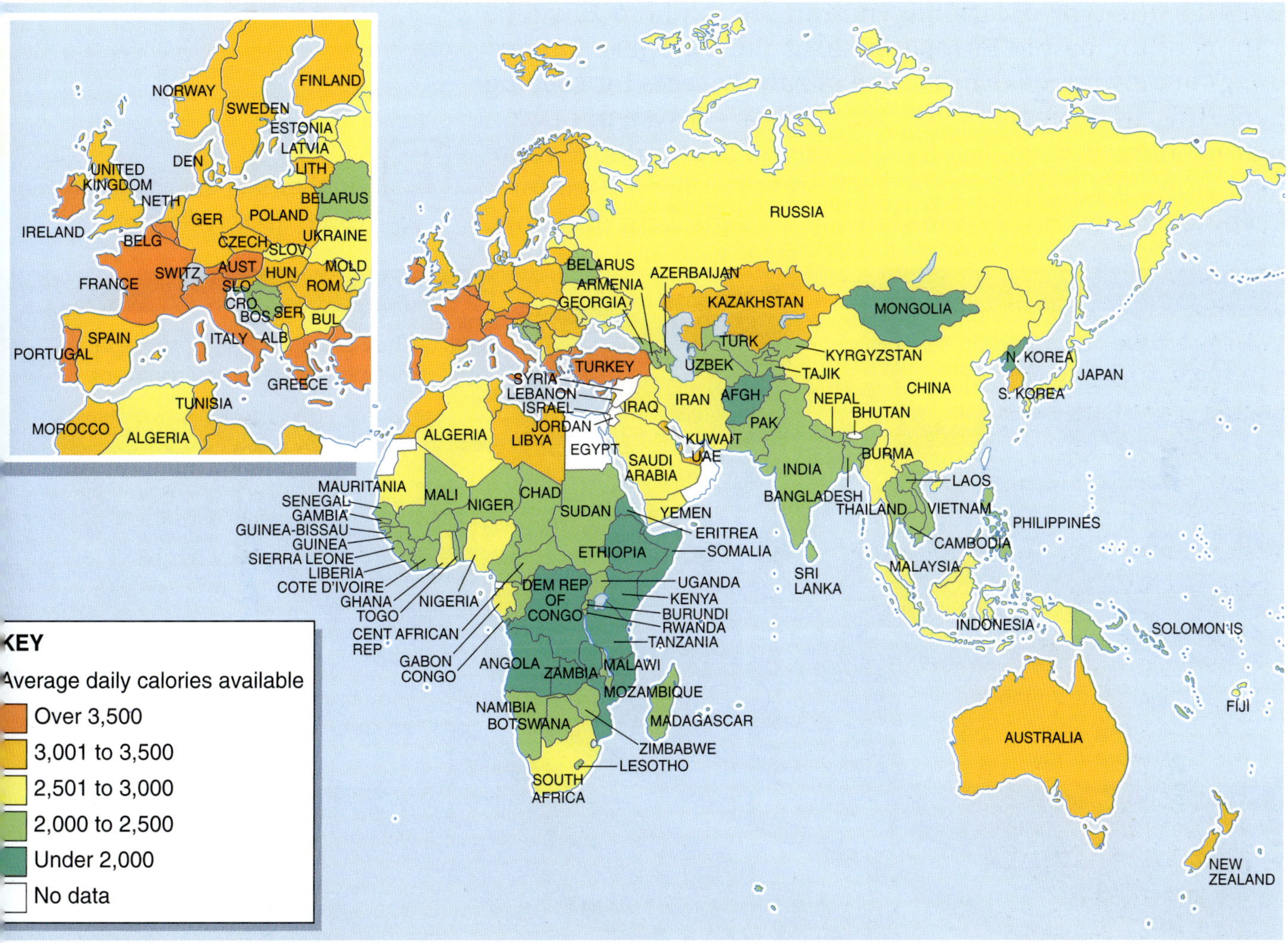

WHAT ARE THE INGREDIENTS FOR A BETTER WORLD?

KEY
Average daily calories available
- Over 3,500
- 3,001 to 3,500
- 2,501 to 3,000
- 2,000 to 2,500
- Under 2,000
- No data

Source: The Atlas of Food, Earthscan 2002

activity...

1. Look at map **C**.
   a) Name five countries where people are more likely to be:
      i) underfed ii) overfed.
   b) Describe the pattern on the map.
      Most of the underfed countries...
      Most of the overfed countries...
2. Look at graph **D**.
   a) Describe what the graph shows.
   b) How does the graph help to explain why some people go hungry when the world has enough food for everyone?

your recipe...

Look again at your recipe. Work out what the calorie content of your meal would be. Your teacher will give you a sheet to do this, or you could use a calorie counter website such as www.thecaloriecounter.com.

Remember, your daily calorie intake should be between 2000 and 2500. Do you want to change the number of calories in your recipe? You can do this by changing the quantities or by changing the ingredients. (For example, you could use semi-skimmed milk rather than whole milk.) If necessary, rewrite your recipe.

FOOD FOR THE FUTURE

➜ Meat on the menu?

By 2012, the type of farming you can see in photo **E** will be a thing of the past in Europe. In 2012 the European Union brings in new laws to ban the use of battery cages for keeping hens. It is an example of FACTORY FARMING – a system of rearing animals using factory-like methods to produce more food at minimum cost. A similar system has been used for keeping pigs, but cattle and sheep are mostly kept outdoors.

E Egg-laying hens in battery cages (factory farming)

- Animals have little freedom to roam or even to exercise
- They produce lots of sewage that pollutes the environment
- Lights are left on longer to encourage hens to lay more eggs
- They cannot behave naturally, so get more pain and health problems
- In cramped conditions they easily catch diseases (these can be passed on to humans)
- Farmers use antibiotics to combat disease (this is making humans resistant to antibiotics)

activity...

1 Look at photo **E**.
  a) Why do you think some farmers keep animals like this?
  b) Do you agree with the EU ban on this type of farming? Why, or why not?

2 Compare photos **E** and **F**.
  a) What are the benefits for the animals of the method of farming in photo **F**? (Use the labels in photo **E** for ideas.)
  b) Why might this method cost more?
  c) Would there be any benefits for consumers? If so, what?

WHAT ARE THE INGREDIENTS FOR A BETTER WORLD?

In Britain, campaigns against factory farming methods have changed public opinion. Many people now think factory farming is cruel. Free-range meat and eggs are more popular. The Freedom Food label provides a guarantee to consumers that the animals have been well treated.

Worldwide, most people still live on a mainly VEGETARIAN diet. However, as countries get richer the amount of meat that people eat increases. In Britain most of us eat meat.

Meat is very costly to produce. Farmers grow huge amounts of grain simply to feed the animals. Three-quarters of farmland in Europe is used to produce animal feed.

F Free-range hens enjoy life outdoors

G Comparing a vegetarian diet and a meat diet

3 Look at source **G**. Explain why a meat diet:
 a) uses more land and energy than a vegetarian diet
 b) is more costly.

your recipe...

Look again at your recipe. Does it include meat or eggs? Having studied these two pages, consider how much meat you are using. Do you want to use the Freedom Food label? If necessary, rewrite your recipe.

FOOD FOR THE FUTURE

➡ Farm inspection

The cheap and plentiful food that we enjoy in Britain comes at a cost. Farms use chemical inputs (like FERTILISERS and PESTICIDES) to increase production. There are concerns about the effect of these on people's health. For example, some pesticides have been linked with cancer.

ORGANIC FARMING uses more traditional farming methods that don't depend on chemicals. Many shops now offer a choice between food that is produced organically, and food that is not. Most of the organic food in the shops carries the Soil Association label. The Soil Association is the organisation that sets the standards for organic food in the UK and inspects farms to ensure the standards are met (**H**).

 Organic food standards

For growing **crops**:
- prohibited (forbidden) methods:
  - the use of chemical herbicides (to kill weeds) and chemical pesticides (to kill insects)
  - the use of chemical fertilisers
  - the use of seeds treated with chemicals
  - growing the same crop continuously on the same land.
- permitted (allowed) methods:
  - the use of pesticides made from plants or minerals
  - weeding with a machine
  - the use of organic seeds
  - the use of natural fertiliser (like animal manure)
  - CROP ROTATION (changing crops between fields from year to year).

For raising **animals**:
- prohibited methods:
  - keeping animals indoors all year round in overcrowded conditions
  - the regular use of drugs to make animals grow, or antibiotics to prevent illness.
- permitted methods:
  - keeping animals indoors for part of the year with fresh air, daylight and space
  - only giving them antibiotics when they are ill.

 A box of organic vegetables

activity...

1 Look at the organic vegetables in photo **I**.
  a) Do they look any different from other vegetables you can buy in the shops? If so, how?
  b) Why are some people prepared to pay more for organic food?

WHAT ARE THE INGREDIENTS FOR A BETTER WORLD?

J The farm calendar on a typical MIXED FARM (growing crops and keeping animals)

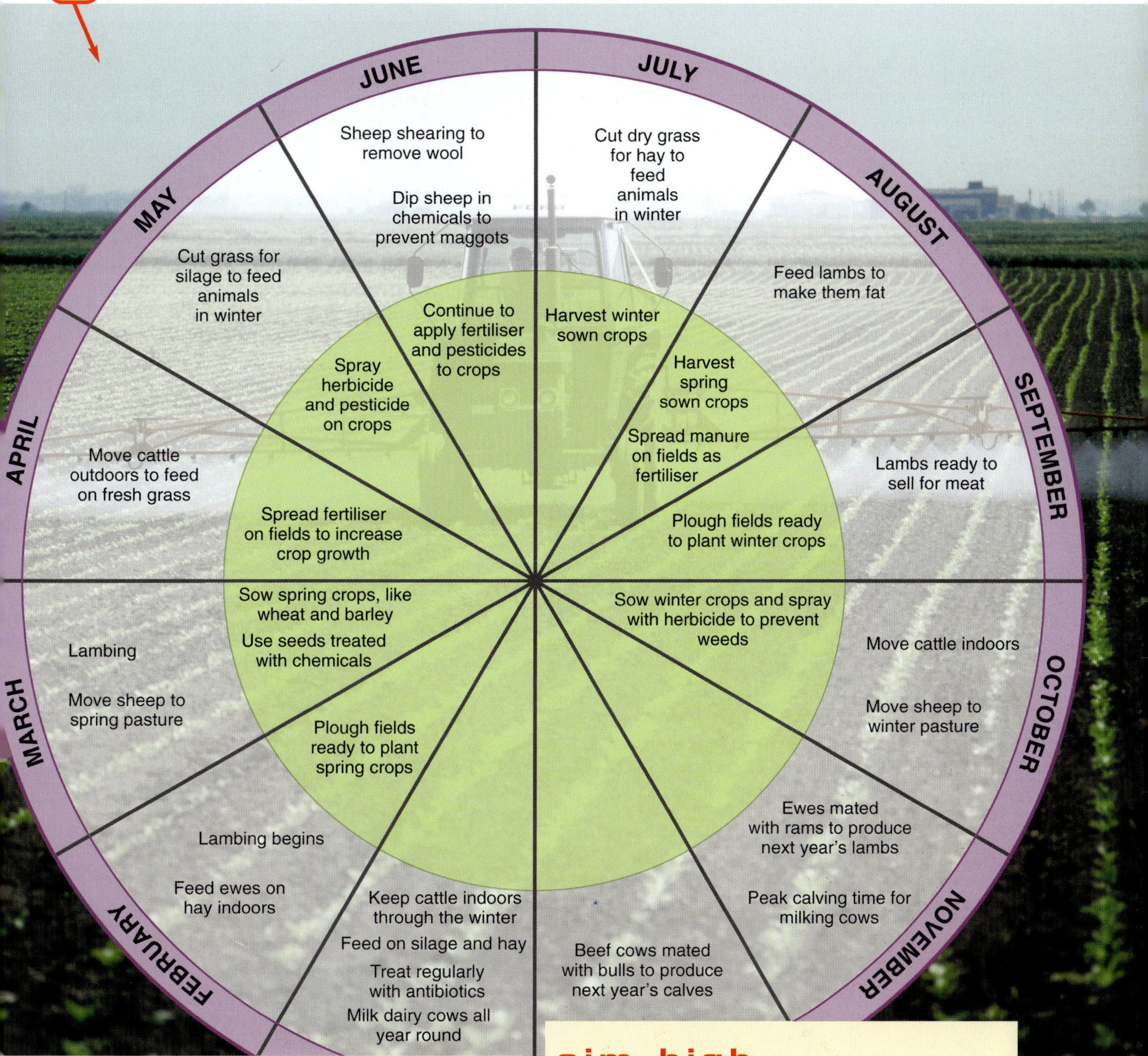

JUNE
- Sheep shearing to remove wool
- Dip sheep in chemicals to prevent maggots
- Continue to apply fertiliser and pesticides to crops
- Spray herbicide and pesticide on crops
- Spread fertiliser on fields to increase crop growth
- Sow spring crops, like wheat and barley
- Use seeds treated with chemicals
- Plough fields ready to plant spring crops

JULY
- Cut dry grass for hay to feed animals in winter
- Harvest winter sown crops
- Harvest spring sown crops
- Spread manure on fields as fertiliser
- Plough fields ready to plant winter crops
- Sow winter crops and spray with herbicide to prevent weeds

MAY
- Cut grass for silage to feed animals in winter

APRIL
- Move cattle outdoors to feed on fresh grass

MARCH
- Lambing
- Move sheep to spring pasture

FEBRUARY
- Lambing begins
- Feed ewes on hay indoors
- Keep cattle indoors through the winter
- Feed on silage and hay
- Treat regularly with antibiotics
- Milk dairy cows all year round

AUGUST
- Feed lambs to make them fat

SEPTEMBER
- Lambs ready to sell for meat

OCTOBER
- Move cattle indoors
- Move sheep to winter pasture

NOVEMBER
- Ewes mated with rams to produce next year's lambs
- Peak calving time for milking cows
- Beef cows mated with bulls to produce next year's calves

2 Read the organic food standards in **H** and then study the farm calendar in **J**. You are a farm inspector from the Soil Association. Which methods would this farm need to change if it wants to produce organic food? Identify five. (You could underline them on a copy of the calendar.)

aim high...

3 For each of the methods that you identified in 2, suggest an alternative method that the farmer could use to produce organic food. For example, *Instead of growing the same crop continuously on the same land, the farmer can use crop rotation.*

75

FOOD FOR THE FUTURE

➡ Down on the (organic) farm

Most of the world farms organically. Farmers in poor countries have been farming like this for centuries, without using chemicals.

Here, in the UK, only four per cent of our farmland is organic. However, the number of organic farms is growing to meet the demand for organic food. At first sight, all farms might look the same, but on closer inspection, organic farms differ from conventional farms (**K**).

The farm uses crop rotation to maintain soil fertility. There are different crops growing in the fields each year. One year a field grows clover and grass for the animals to graze. This gives the soil a rest and clover puts nitrogen back into the soil naturally. Next year, the nitrogen helps the next crop to grow.

Penrhiw Farm, an organic farm in west Wales

It is a mixed farm – growing crops and rearing animals. Most organic farms are mixed. The animals fertilise the soil naturally by adding manure. The farm produces organic crops that can be used to feed the animals. This is more like the balance in nature.

There is more wildlife on the farm because they do not spray chemicals. As a result there are more weeds growing in the fields and insects living in the soil. This encourages more birds and other animals to live on the farm.

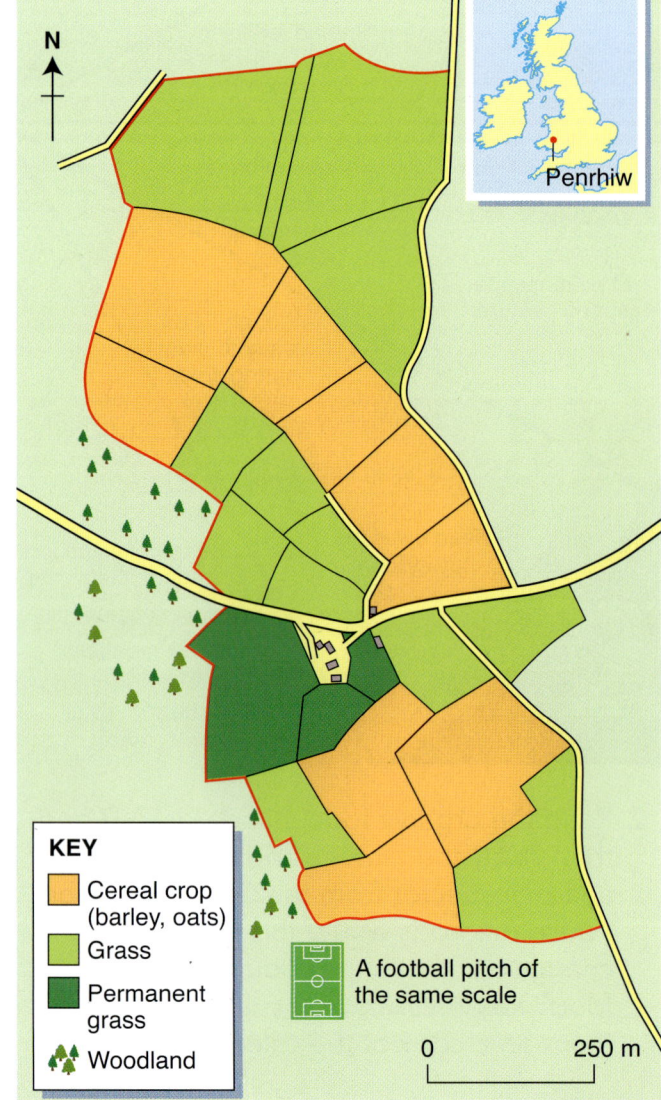

KEY
- Cereal crop (barley, oats)
- Grass
- Permanent grass
- Woodland
- A football pitch of the same scale

0   250 m

WHAT ARE THE INGREDIENTS FOR A BETTER WORLD?

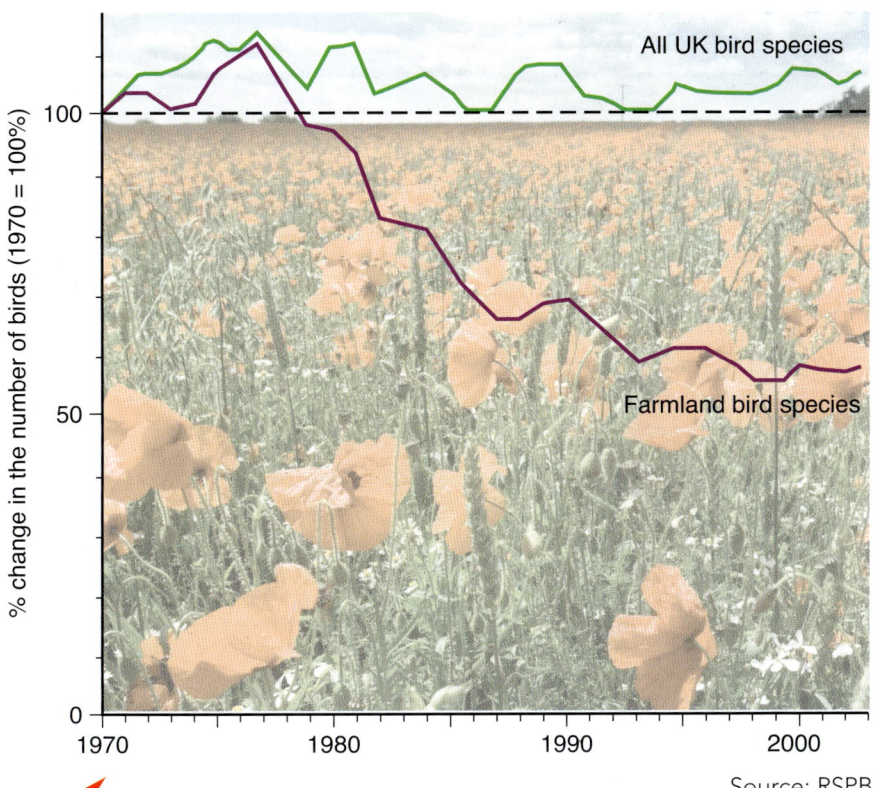

The number of farmland bird species in the UK has dropped sharply since 1970. This has a lot to do with farming methods:

- insecticides reduce the number of insects that birds eat
- herbicides reduce the weeds and seeds that provide food in winter
- growing crops continuously means there are fewer nesting sites for birds.

Research shows that organic farming encourages birds to return. The growth of organic farming may be one reason that the decline in farmland birds has slowed down.

L Bird numbers in the UK since 1970

activity...

1 Many of the differences between organic and conventional farms are hard to spot. On which type of farm (organic or non-organic) would you be most likely to:
  a) hear birds singing?
  b) wear a protective mask?
  c) see no animals grazing?
  d) see poppies growing in the field?
  e) get higher crop yields?
  f) employ more people?
  In each case, give a reason.

2 Look at graph **L**.
  a) Describe carefully how the number of farmland birds has changed. Write three sentences.
     From 1970 until 1980...
     Between 1980 and 2000...
     Since 2000...
  b) How did this compare with the change in the number of all UK birds?
  c) How could farming methods explain what you see on the graph?

aim high...

3 In the shops, organic food usually costs more than ordinary food. From what you have learnt about organic farming, why do you think this is? Give at least two reasons.

your recipe...

Look again at your recipe. Do you include any organic ingredients? Does it matter whether your ingredients are organic or not?

Compare the prices of organic food and ordinary food in the supermarket. How much more would your meal cost if you use organic ingredients? Is it worth paying the extra money, do you think?

If necessary, rewrite your recipe. Specify the ingredients that should be organic.

FOOD FOR THE FUTURE

→Chocolate unwrapped

There's one thing we nearly all eat. Chocolate! On average, in the UK, we eat about 10 kg of chocolate every year and spend £1.33 a week each on it. Chocolate with lots of cocoa in it (70% plus) is good for us as a treat. But we all know that too much chocolate is unhealthy. Did you know that chocolate can be bad for the people who produce it too? Some cocoa farmers in Ghana earn less each week than the average UK family spends on chocolate.

M What is in a bar of chocolate?

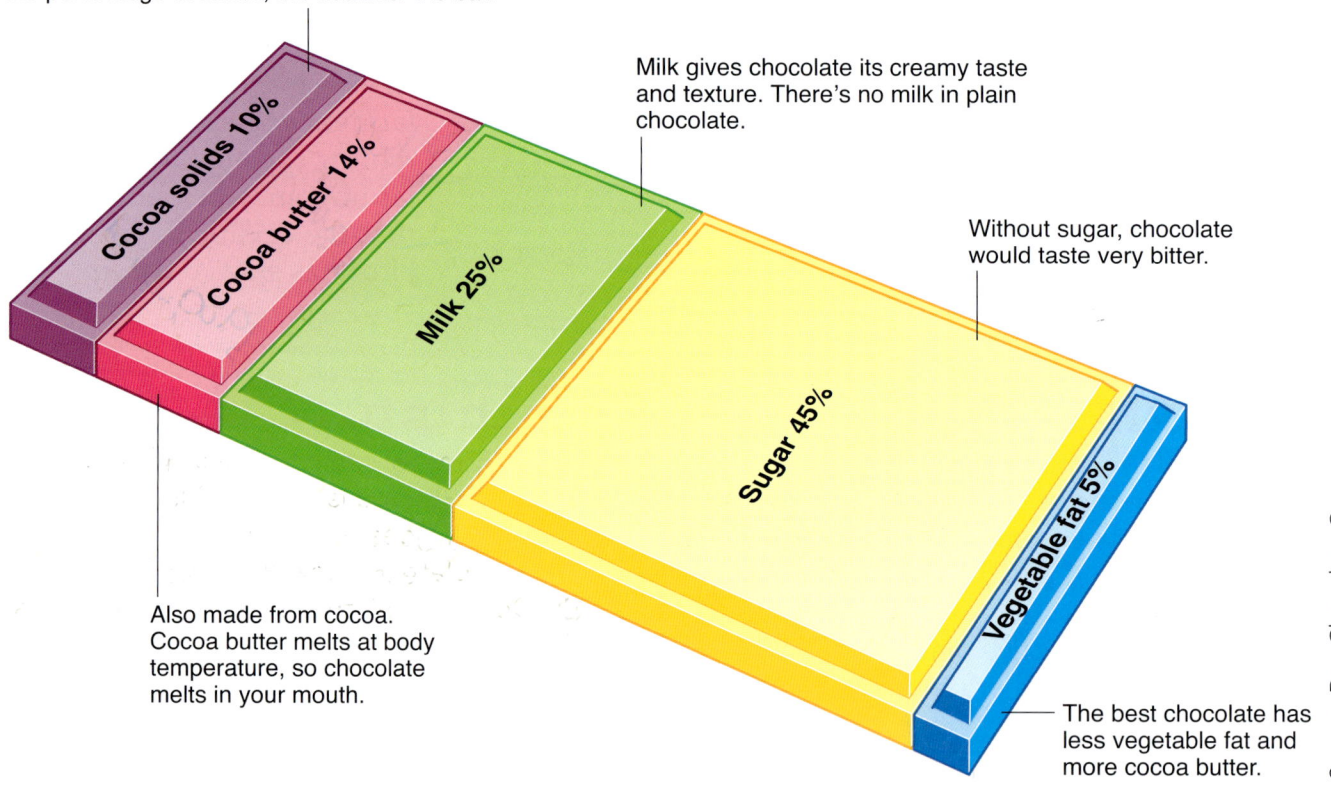

Cocoa gives chocolate its rich taste. The higher the percentage of cocoa, the healthier the bar.

Milk gives chocolate its creamy taste and texture. There's no milk in plain chocolate.

Without sugar, chocolate would taste very bitter.

Also made from cocoa. Cocoa butter melts at body temperature, so chocolate melts in your mouth.

The best chocolate has less vegetable fat and more cocoa butter.

Source: Day Chocolate Company

Cocoa trees produce large pods that contain cocoa beans. It takes five years to produce the first crop after planting.

To harvest the cocoa, chop the pods from the tree, then split them open. Scrape out the cocoa beans.

Wrap the beans in leaves and leave them in the sun for a week to allow the chocolatey flavour to develop. Then spread them out to dry.

WHAT ARE THE INGREDIENTS FOR A BETTER WORLD?

Top five producers	tonnes (1000s)
Cote d'Ivoire	1,407
Ghana	737
Indonesia	430
Nigeria	180
Cameroon	162

Top five consumers	tonnes (1000s)
USA	775
Germany	289
France	230
UK	220
Russia	177

Source: The Economist Pocket Book of Figures 2007

  The world's top cocoa producers and consumers

activity...

1 Look at the pictures in **N**. List the jobs that each of these would do;
 a) the cocoa farmer   c) the chocolate company
 b) the cocoa exporter   d) the supermarket
2 Look at the tables in **O**. Find the countries on a world map. Write two sentences to describe the location of:
 a) cocoa producing countries
 b) cocoa consuming countries.
 Which continents are they in? Are they MEDCs or LEDCs? (Look back at page 54 if you can't remember what these are.)
3 Look at the diagram on the right. It shows who earns what from a £1 bar of chocolate.
 a) Who gets most money? Who gets least?
 b) Who has the hardest job, do you think? (Look back at activity 1.)
 c) How much money stays in LEDCs (where cocoa is grown)? How much money goes to MEDCs (where chocolate is made and sold)?
 d) Do you think this is fair? Give reasons.

Source: Xchanging the world. Reading International Solidarity Centre

  From cocoa bean to chocolate bar

Grade the beans and weigh them in sacks ready to be exported.

Ship the beans to a chocolate factory in the UK. Then roast them, squash them, and mix the cocoa with milk and sugar.

Cool the chocolate in a mould, wrap it and send it to supermarkets to be sold.

Ups and downs for a cocoa farmer

This is Mim, a village in Ghana where cocoa is grown. Most of the families who live here earn their living by growing cocoa.

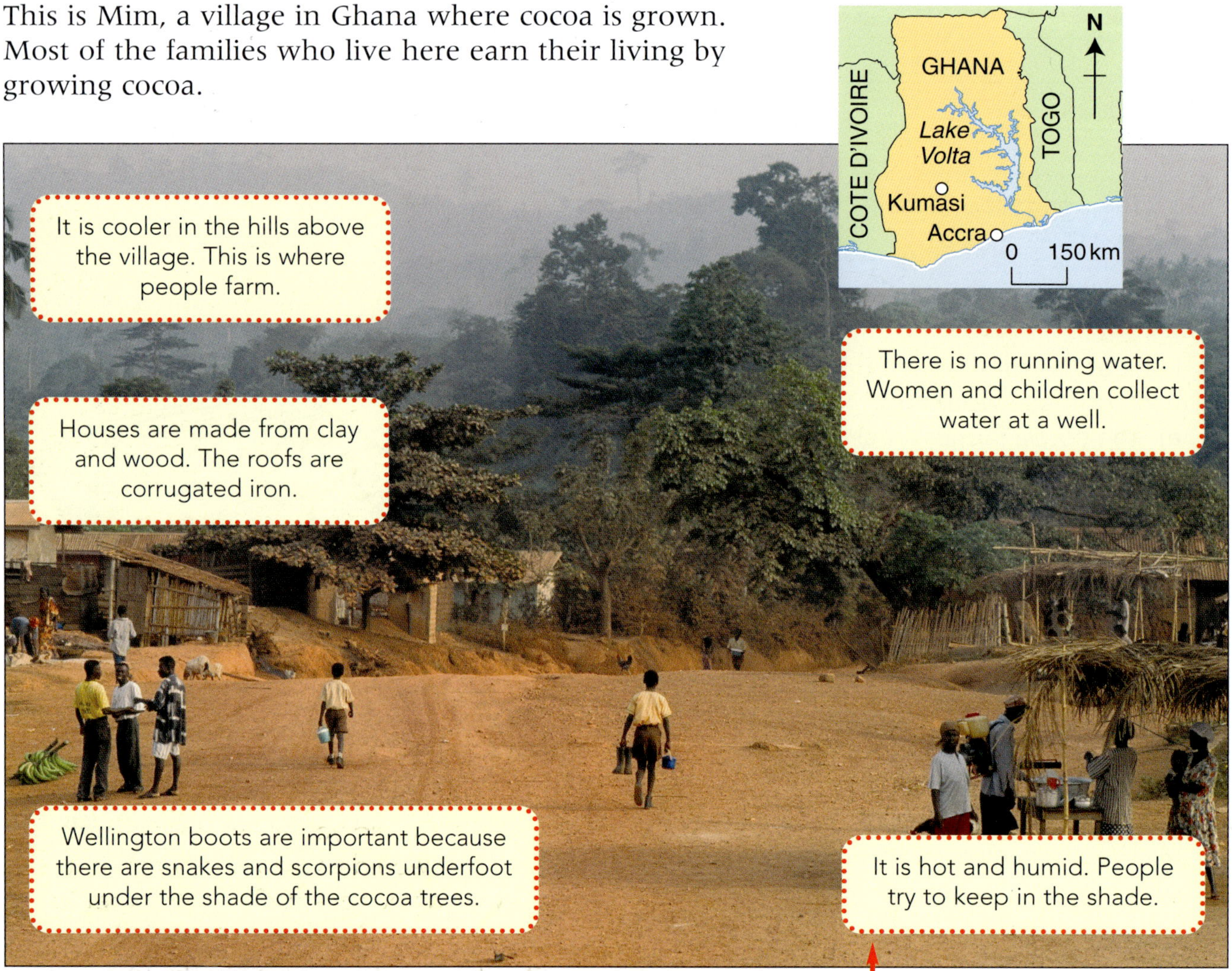
N
GHANA
COTE D'IVOIRE
TOGO
Lake Volta
Kumasi
Accra
0 150 km
It is cooler in the hills above the village. This is where people farm.
Houses are made from clay and wood. The roofs are corrugated iron.
There is no running water. Women and children collect water at a well.
Wellington boots are important because there are snakes and scorpions underfoot under the shade of the cocoa trees.
It is hot and humid. People try to keep in the shade.

P The village of Mim on the road to Kumasi

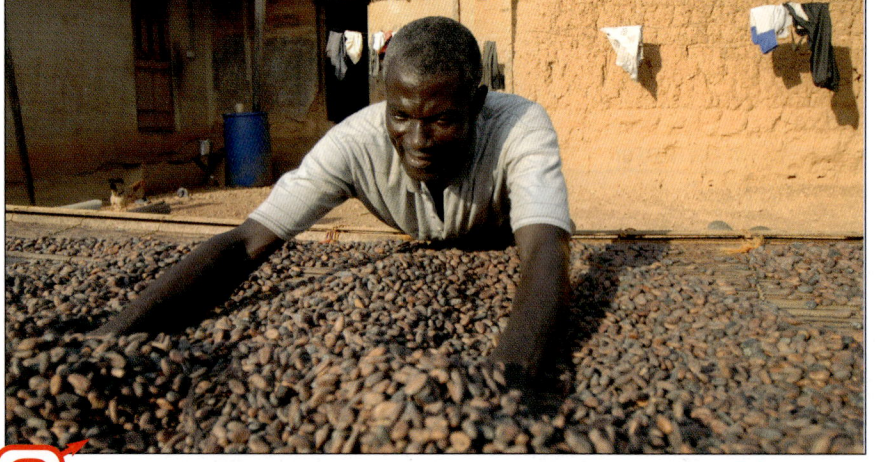

Q Francis is a cocoa farmer in Mim. He grows cocoa to sell, and vegetables to feed his family. A typical smallholder cocoa farmer in Ghana earns around £300 a year from growing cocoa. That works out at just 82p per day!

The money cocoa farmers earn depends on the WORLD MARKET PRICE for cocoa. This is fixed by traders in cities, like London or New York, thousands of miles from Ghana. When there is a shortage of cocoa, the price rises; and when there is a surplus, it falls (graph **R**).

WHAT ARE THE INGREDIENTS FOR A BETTER WORLD?

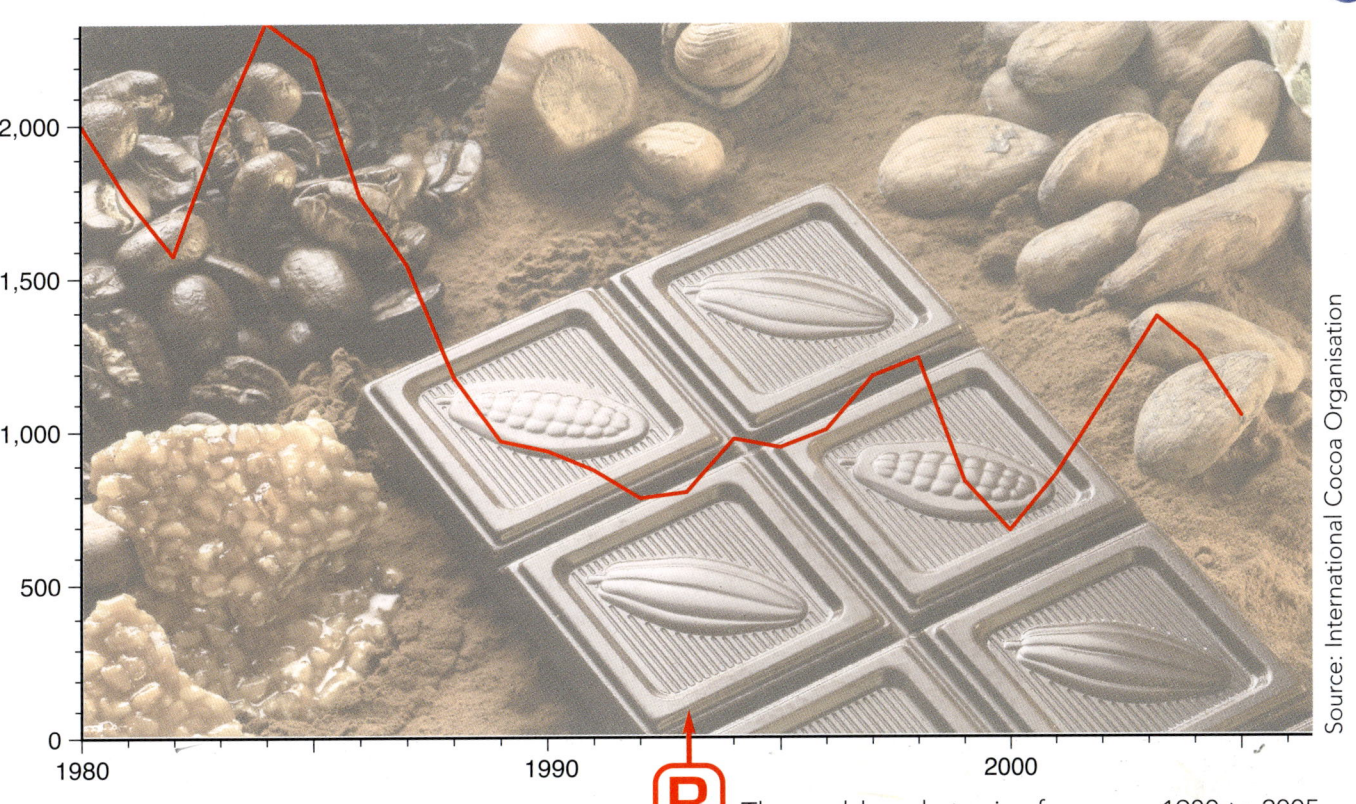

R The world market price for cocoa 1980 to 2005

Source: International Cocoa Organisation

activity...

1 You are going to find out how difficult is it for Francis and his family to survive on £300 a year (£25 a month). They have three children, one at secondary school.
   a) Read this list of prices in Ghana.

Monthly secondary school fees (per child)	£4.00
Loaf of bread	50p
Bottle of cooking oil	£1.40
Sack of maize (feeds a family for a month)	£21.60
Bus ride to the city	£7.00
Big bar of soap	50p
Trip to hospital to treat malaria (can happen any time)	£4.00
Pair of wellington boots	£4.00
New school uniform	£2.00
Radio	£2.90
Battery (for radio)	30p
Bar of chocolate	87p

   b) Plan a monthly budget for Francis's family. Remember you only have £25. What would you spend money on? What would you do without? What would you save for? (Don't forget to include saving in your budget.)
   c) What will happen when the two other children reach secondary school age?

2 Look at graph R.
   a) What was the price of cocoa in i) 1980 and ii) 2005?
   b) How would you describe cocoa prices between 1980 and 2005?
   c) How does the world cocoa price affect Francis?
   d) Does Francis feel confident about the future, do you think? Why?

3 What could you do to help Francis – give up eating chocolate or eat even more? Explain your answer.

FOOD FOR THE FUTURE

→ The chocolate choice

Cocoa farmers in Ghana have been getting poorer, while people around the world eat more chocolate and the companies selling chocolate make big profits. How fair is that?

It is MEDCs like Britain that control international trade. They charge high taxes to import PROCESSED GOODS (like chocolate), but low taxes to import RAW MATERIALS (like cocoa). This prevents LEDCs (like Ghana) having their own factories, and forces them to produce raw materials. As the supply of raw materials grows, the world market price falls.

Cocoa farmers in Ghana are caught in a trap. The more cocoa they produce the less they get paid for it. But there is another way. It is called FAIR TRADE.

 The Kuapa Kokoo Co-operative is an association of cocoa farmers in Ghana. It sells cocoa and is run on fair trade principles

		Kuapa Kokoo farmers	Non-Kuapa Kokoo farmers
How the cocoa beans are weighed		They are weighed on accurate scales. Kuapa Kokoo exports the beans directly.	The buyers weigh the beans on their own scales before they buy them. Sometimes the buyers are dishonest. They sell the beans to the exporters.
Local price for cocoa beans		Farmers receive a higher share of the price for their beans. There is no one else in the trading chain to share the money.	Farmers get a lower share of the price for their beans. There are more people in the trading chain to share the money.
World price for cocoa beans		Kuapa Kokoo receives a guaranteed price ($1,600 per tonne) by selling to fair trade companies like Day Chocolate Company.	The price farmers receive goes up and down with the world market price. In recent years the price has fallen to $1,000 per tonne.
How profits are shared		Profits are shared equally between farmers at the end of the year. Kuapa Kokoo also owns one third of Day Chocolate Company so farmers receive extra profits.	Farmers barely cover their costs so there is no profit. They do not share any of the profit the chocolate companies make.
Other benefits for farmers and community		Farmers are given free training and education. Fair trade companies pay a bonus of $150 per tonne of beans for community projects, like new drinking wells.	No training or education for farmers. No bonus.

WHAT ARE THE INGREDIENTS FOR A BETTER WORLD?

Fairtrade aims to change the rules of international trade. The Fairtrade Foundation in the UK was set up to ensure a better deal for producers in LEDCs. The FAIRTRADE Mark guarantees:
- better prices
- decent working conditions
- local sustainability
- fair terms of trade for producers in LEDCs.

In addition to Fairtrade chocolate, it is possible to buy Fairtrade tea, coffee, sugar, bananas, honey, rice and many other products. Look out for them when you shop.

investigate...

You are going to investigate Fairtrade at your local supermarket.

1. How many Fairtrade products can you find? (Look for the FAIRTRADE Mark.) Make a list.
2. a) Compare the price of the Fairtrade products on your list with an equivalent non-Fairtrade product. Is there any price difference?
   b) If so, how do you explain it?

aim high...

3. Survey adults you know who shop, to find out if they support Fairtrade.
   a) Design a simple questionnaire that you can use for your survey. You need to find out:
      - do they recognise the FAIRTRADE Mark?
      - do they know what Fairtrade is?
      - would they be prepared to choose Fairtrade?
   b) Carry out your survey. Talk to at least five adults. You may need to:
      - show them the FAIRTRADE Mark
      - explain what Fairtrade is
      - tell them some prices.
   c) Write a conclusion to your survey to answer the question: 'Is there support for Fairtrade among shoppers?'

your recipe...

Look again at your recipe. Is chocolate one of your ingredients? If not, what about other ingredients, like bananas, rice or honey?

Does it matter if you use Fairtrade ingredients or not? How much would your meal cost if you used Fairtrade ingredients? If necessary, rewrite your recipe. Specify the ingredients that could be Fairtrade.

83

FOOD FOR THE FUTURE

➡ Ready, steady, cook!

The government wants every secondary school pupil to learn to cook. It is important that we learn to cook when we are young, so that we stay healthy for the rest of our lives. It is more difficult to eat and stay healthy when you only eat food from a packet or takeaway meals. You don't know what ingredients they put in them.

Through this unit you have been asking other questions about ingredients: 'How many food miles?' 'How many calories?' 'Meat or vegetarian?' 'Organic or not?' 'Fairtrade or not?' These are important questions to ask if what you eat is to be good, not just for you but for the world too.

discuss...

Look back at the work you have done through this unit. For each of the questions you asked through this unit, think about why it is an important question to ask. For example, *How many food miles? The number of food miles our food travels affects the environment. The more miles it travels, the more fuel we burn and the more carbon emissions we produce. This adds to global warming.*

a) How many food miles?

b) How many calories?

c) Meat or vegetarian?

d) Organic or not?

e) Fairtrade or not?

THE OLYMPIC GAMES AND PARALYMPIC GAMES COME TO TOWN

activity...

1. Look at photo **B**.
   a) Use the scale to work out the size of the site in hectares or km² (100 ha = 1 km²). The easiest way is to place a hectare grid over the photo and count the squares.
   b) What advantages did this site have for the Olympic Games? Mention its size, previous land use and its location.

your bid...

2. Look at an aerial photo or map of your nearest city. If you live in London, look at another part of the city. Identify a suitable site for an Olympic Park. It should be:
   a) a similar size to the Stratford site
   b) mainly unused wasteland
   c) easily accessible from the city centre.

aim high...

3. Draw a plan for your own Olympic Park, to fit the site you have chosen in 2.

THE OLYMPIC GAMES AND PARALYMPIC GAMES COME TO TOWN

→ Olympic venues

Most of the venues for the 2012 Olympic Games are in and around London (map **E**). Football and sailing will happen at venues further from the capital (map **D**). Nearly all the action is concentrated in two areas of east London – the Olympic Park in Stratford (map **F**) and the River Zone around the River Thames and the Docks (map **G**).

Horse Guards Parade, the venue for beach volleyball

THE OLYMPIC GAMES AND PARALYMPIC GAMES COME TO TOWN

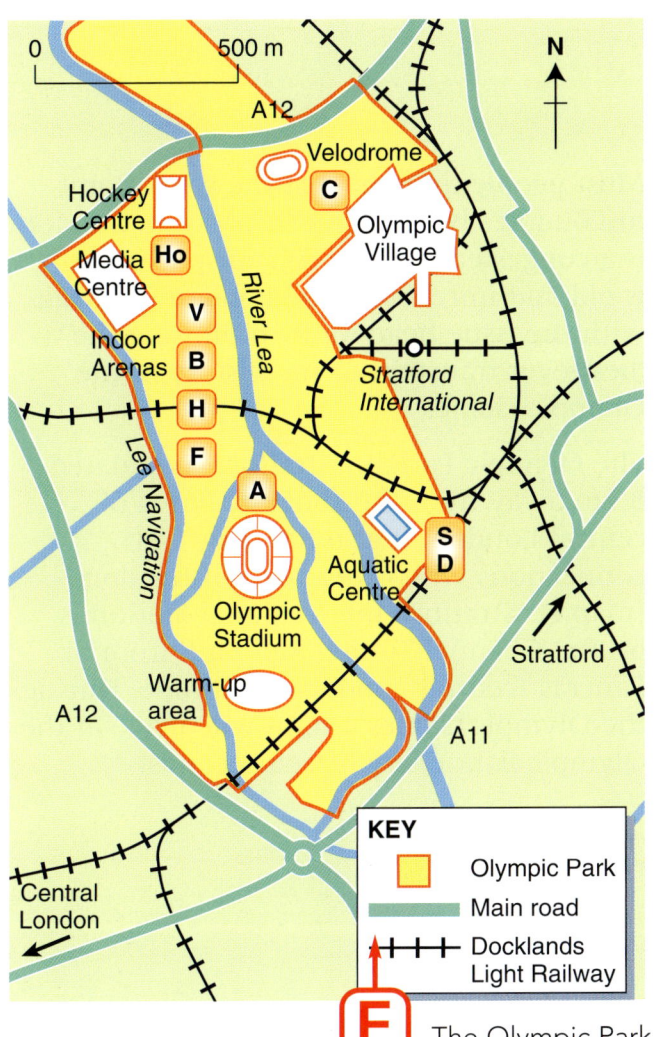

F The Olympic Park

activity...
1 Study the maps on this spread to find out where all the Olympic events will happen. Make a list.

your bid...
2 You have already chosen the site for your Olympic Park. Many of the events will happen here.
   a) Now, think of suitable venues for other sports, in and around your city.
   b) Mark them on a map of your city. Give the map a key.

A	Athletics	F	Football	So	Softball
Ar	Archery	Fe	Fencing	T	Tennis
B	Basketball	G	Gymnastics	Tr	Triathlon
Ba	Badminton	H	Handball	Tt	Table tennis
Bo	Boxing	Ho	Hockey	V	Volleyball
Bb	Baseball	M	Martial arts	Vb	Beach volleyball
C	Cycling	P	Pentathlon	W	Weightlifting
Ca	Canoeing	S	Swimming	Wp	Water polo
D	Diving	Sa	Sailing	Wr	Wrestling
E	Equestrian	Sh	Shooting		

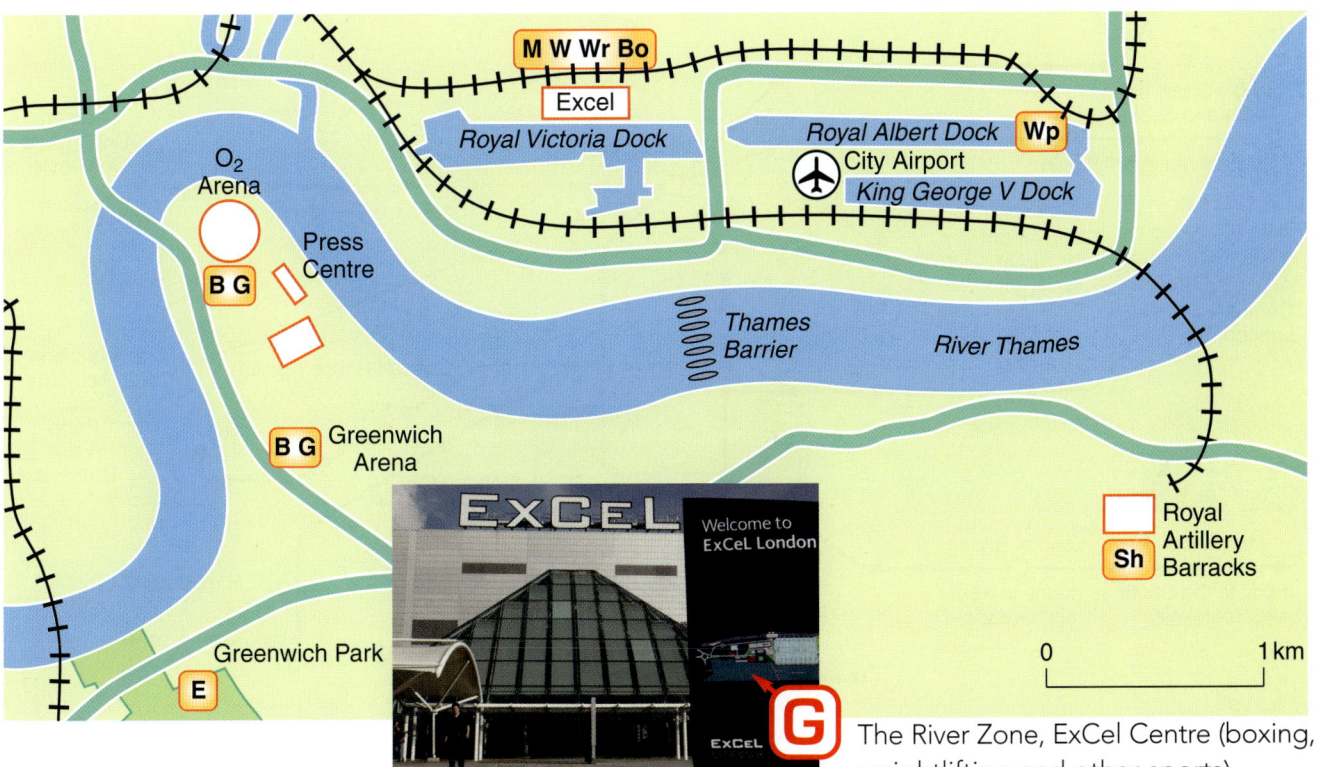

G The River Zone, ExCeL Centre (boxing, weightlifting and other sports)

THE OLYMPIC GAMES AND PARALYMPIC GAMES COME TO TOWN

→ Best-ever games transport

H Congestion in central London

Most people thought that the weak point in London's bid would be transport. London is a congested city and its transport system is old and unreliable. The London bid dealt with the issue head on by promising the 'best-ever transport in the history of the Olympic Games'.

The Olympic Park, in Stratford, is situated 8 km away from the congested area of central London. It also has good rail connections with other parts of London (map **I**). Stratford International Station is on the Channel Tunnel Rail Link from St Pancras (central London) to Europe. During the Olympic Games a train will arrive at the Olympic Park every fifteen seconds!

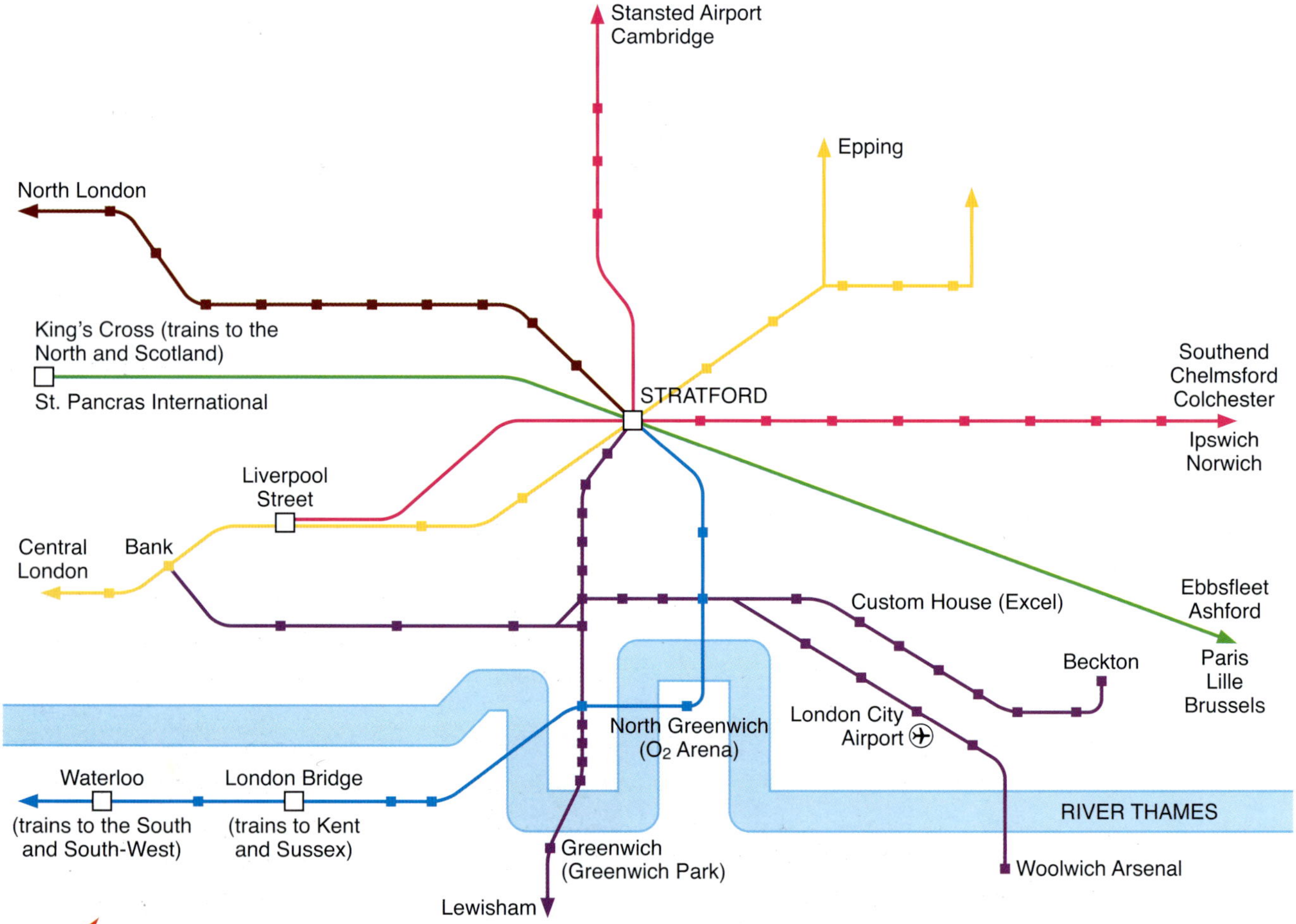

I Rail connections to Stratford

THE OLYMPIC GAMES AND PARALYMPIC GAMES COME TO TOWN

The new Channel Tunnel Rail Link route from St Pancras to Stratford will allow passengers to reach the Olympic Park within seven minutes on arriving in London. They will use the Olympic Javelin, a high-speed shuttle service (photo **K**). A similar service will operate from Kent to Stratford for passengers coming from Europe (map **J**).

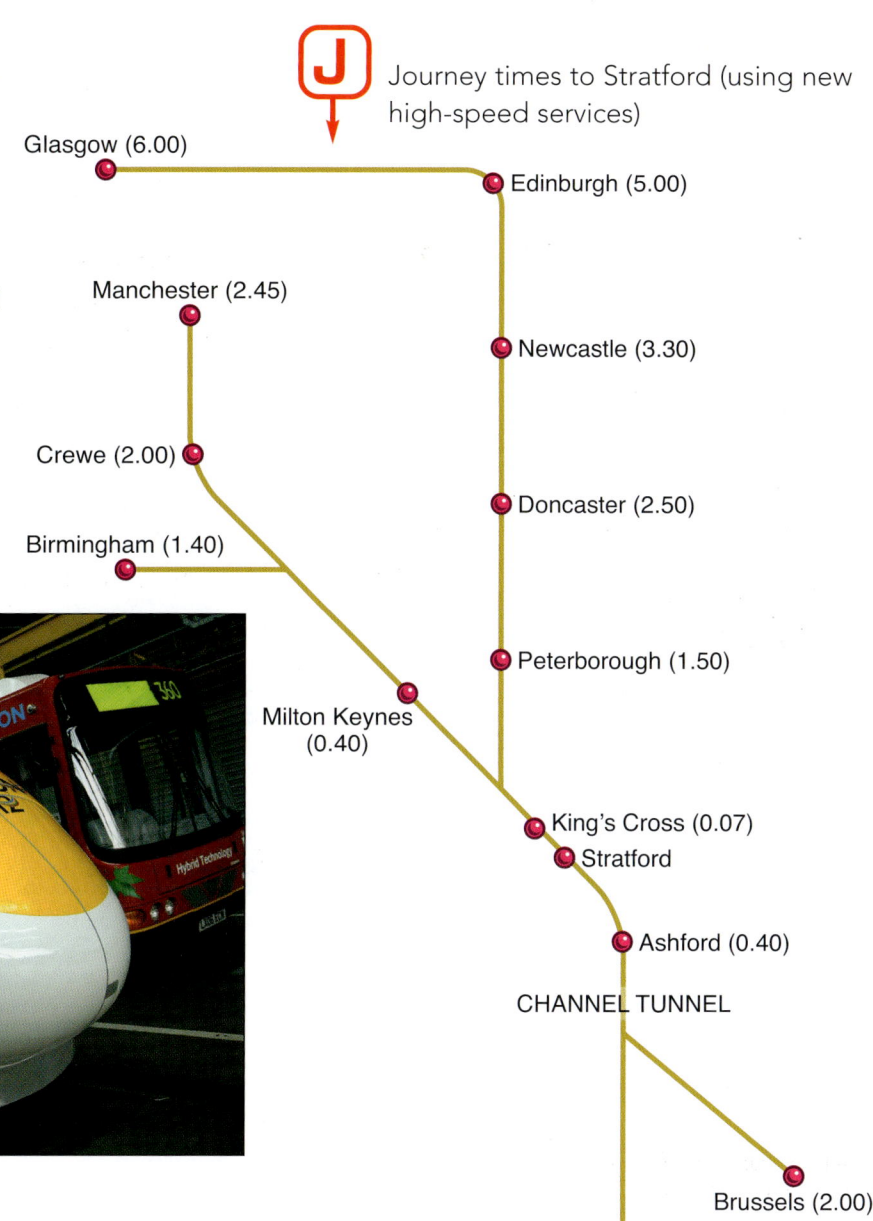

J Journey times to Stratford (using new high-speed services)

- Glasgow (6.00)
- Edinburgh (5.00)
- Manchester (2.45)
- Newcastle (3.30)
- Crewe (2.00)
- Doncaster (2.50)
- Birmingham (1.40)
- Peterborough (1.50)
- Milton Keynes (0.40)
- King's Cross (0.07)
- Stratford
- Ashford (0.40)
- CHANNEL TUNNEL
- Brussels (2.00)
- Paris (2.20)

K The Olympic Javelin

activity...

1. Look at map **I**. Use it to plan some journeys in London for the Olympic Games
   a) Which lines would you use to get to Stratford from,
      i) King's Cross   ii) Waterloo   iii) Liverpool Street
   b) How would you get to four other Olympic venues from Stratford? Describe the route you would use.
2. Plan a rail journey to the Olympic Park from where you live.
   a) Use the maps on this spread to help you to plan your journey. At which station would you arrive in London? How would you get to Stratford? Roughly, how long would the whole journey take?
   b) What are the advantages of travelling by rail (for you and for the environment)?

your bid...

3. a) What rail links does your city have? Draw a map to show these links.
   b) What improvements would you plan for transport in and around your city before you make your Games bid?

THE OLYMPIC GAMES AND PARALYMPIC GAMES COME TO TOWN

➔ A sustainable games

L Lea Valley, before work began on the Olympic Park

The Olympic Park is situated in the Lower Lea Valley, one of London's least developed areas. Before work began on the Olympic Park, the river and canal network were choked by weeds and rubbish. The surrounding land was a mixture of old factories, scrap yards and wasteland (photo **L**).

With the Olympic Games, the valley is set to become a model of SUSTAINABLE DEVELOPMENT. The aim is to restore the environment and to improve the quality of life for local communities in a way that will outlast the Games in 2012 (source **M**).

activity...

1. 'Sustainable' and 'development' are two words you have already met in Geography.
   a) Write down a meaning for each word. If you are not sure, or if you have forgotten, check the glossary on pages 139–140.
   b) What do you think 'sustainable development' means? Write down your own meaning. Then check the glossary and change it if you need to (you might prefer your own meaning!).
2. Study the information in **M**.
   a) Choose at least five ways in which the Olympic Park is an example of sustainable development. For example,
      More than 80% of journeys to and from the Park will be by rail.
   b) Draw a large spider diagram like the one on the right to fill a page in your book. Write your examples of sustainable development at the end of each line.
   c) Now, on each line, explain how your examples show sustainable development. For example,
      Travelling by rail causes less congestion and pollution.

your bid...

3. Think how you would organise a sustainable Olympic Games in your city. You could use some of the ideas from the London Games bid, but you can include ideas of your own. For example, you could restore a disused mining area rather than a valley. Make a list of your ideas.

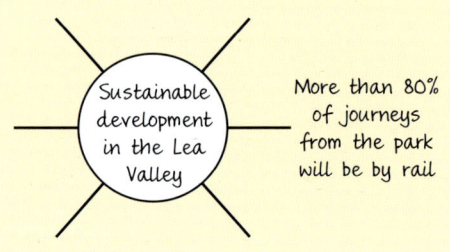

THE OLYMPIC GAMES AND PARALYMPIC GAMES COME TO TOWN

A valley reborn
- The area of wasteland will be transformed into one of the largest urban parks in Europe.
- A network of footpaths and cycleways will link communities on either side of the valley.
- The park will be planted with trees to provide a home for wildlife.

Planning for sustainability
- The Olympic village will provide accommodation for 17,000 athletes. After the Olympic Games these will be turned into homes for local people.
- Accommodation will be within easy walking distance of amenities, including shops and schools.
- All facilities will also be accessible for wheelchair users.

Olympic Park

Lee Navigation

River Lea

River Thames

N

0   500 m

A zero-waste Games
- Companies that provide materials, services and food for the Olympic Games will be required to produce minimum waste.
- There will be recycling facilities at every venue.
- Waste material that can't be recycled will be used as an energy source.

A low-carbon Games
- More than 80% of journeys to and from the Olympic Park will be by rail.
- Visitors from Europe will be able to travel direct to Stratford rather than use a plane.
- New buses to the Olympic Park will be low emission vehicles.

Sustainable development of the Lower Lea Valley

THE OLYMPIC GAMES AND PARALYMPIC GAMES COME TO TOWN

➜ A lasting legacy

The boroughs around the Lower Lea Valley are among the most deprived, not only in London, but also in the UK. Factory closures and the loss of jobs have led to the high levels of UNEMPLOYMENT (map **N**). The Olympic Games could help to change that. The Olympic Park is expected to regenerate the area by creating 12,000 new jobs in work like construction, tourism and the media.

Unemployment in London boroughs

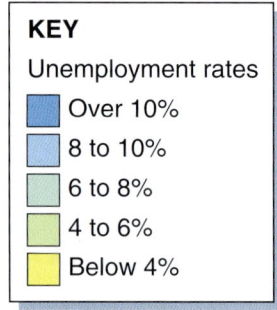

KEY
Unemployment rates
- Over 10%
- 8 to 10%
- 6 to 8%
- 4 to 6%
- Below 4%

KEY
1. Hammersmith and Fulham
2. Kensington and Chelsea
3. Westminster
4. Islington
5. City
6. Tower Hamlets

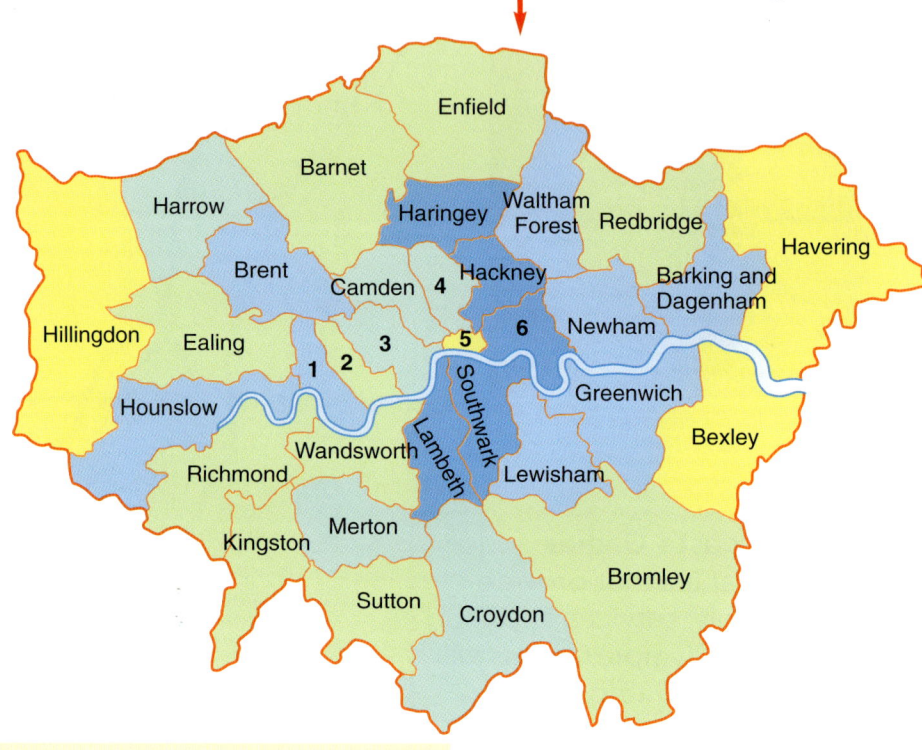

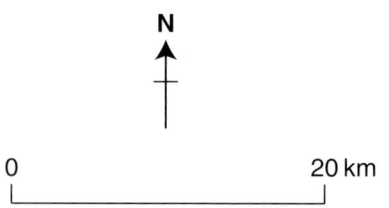

activity...

1. Look at map **N**.
   a) What is the unemployment rate in Newham (the borough where Stratford is)?
   b) How does it compare with other boroughs in London?
   c) Write one or two sentences to describe the pattern on the map.
2. You are going to make a concept map to show how indicators of DEPRIVATION are linked.
   a) Write seven indicators of deprivation on a whole page in your book, as shown on the right.
   b) Draw lines between any of the indicators that you think are linked. For example, *employment and income.*
   c) Write a sentence on each line you draw to explain the link. For example, *Income depends on the job you do. If you are unemployed your income is very low.*

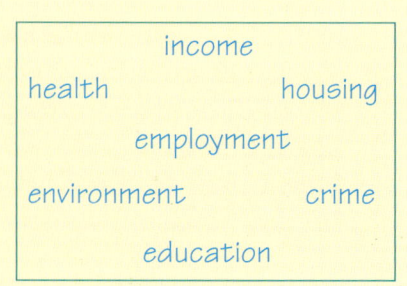

THE OLYMPIC GAMES AND PARALYMPIC GAMES COME TO TOWN

Deprivation is about what is lacking in an area. Seven indicators are used to measure levels of deprivation:
- employment
- health
- crime
- education
- income
- housing
- environment

By comparing these indicators of deprivation, the most deprived areas in England are:

England rank	London rank	Area
1	-	Liverpool
2	-	Manchester
3	-	Knowsley
4	1	Tower Hamlets
5	2	Hackney
6	3	Islington
7	-	Nottingham
8	-	Easington
9	-	Hull
10	-	Middlesbrough
11	4	Newham

P The most deprived areas in England

your bid...

3 Find out about deprivation in your city. Can you find out about any of the indicators of deprivation shown in source **Q**? You can try the website for your borough or local government, for example www.manchester.gov.uk. How do levels of deprivation in your city compare with other places?

aim high...

4 Think about how the Olympic Games could help to regenerate a city.
   a) Look at the concept map you made in activity 2. Which indicators would the Olympic Games affect? How would this happen?
   b) Write a paragraph to explain how the Olympic Games could help to regenerate a city.

Q Comparing Newham with the rest of London

Average income
Newham: £27,600
London: £34,625

Life expectancy (for men)
Newham: 73.7
London: 76.0

Educational qualifications (people with a degree)
Newham: 15.5%
London: 30.8%

Violent crime (violence against the person)
Newham: 32.8 per 1,000 people
London: 25.2 per 1,000 people

Unemployment
Newham: 9.4%
London: 7.0%

Home ownership (households owning the home they live in)
Newham: 42.4%
London: 55.5%

Source: London Borough of Newham

THE OLYMPIC GAMES AND PARALYMPIC GAMES COME TO TOWN

➡ We back the bid

Sixty-eight per cent of Londoners supported London's bid for the Olympic Games. In east London, the support was even greater. There are many reasons for local people to back the bid.

- 17,000 athletes will come here from all over the world. I could be one!
- There will be thousands of new homes. One day I'd like to buy one.
- There are going to be loads of exciting jobs here when I leave school.
- I'll be able to watch the Olympic Games on my doorstep – not on telly!
- The sports facilities will be fantastic.
- We'll be able to do athletics, swimming, cycling, tennis and loads more.
- It's going to boost the area's image. It'll put the East End on the map.
- More people will get into sport. It will be good for our health.
- Transport will improve. London in seven minutes, Paris in two hours!
- We can all get involved in the Games. They need 70,000 volunteers.
- This area is a mess. The Olympic Park will improve the environment.

investigate...

1 Talk to five people who you know.
   a) Ask them if they backed the bid for the London Olympic Games. What was their reason?
   b) Now, ask them if they would back a bid for the Olympic Games in your nearest city. Why?
   c) Share your results with the rest of your class. Between you, you should have a good representative sample of people.
   d) Work out the percentage that would back each bid:
      i) What percentage backed the London bid?
      ii) What percentage would back your city's bid?

discuss...

2 a) Do you think that London was the best choice for a British Games bid?
   b) Is it fair that most national events are held in London? What would be fairer?

THE OLYMPIC GAMES AND PARALYMPIC GAMES COME TO TOWN

your final task...

Here is a summary of the reasons that London's Games bid was successful:

London is the UK capital city. 68% of the population backed the bid.

Stratford has good rail connections with other parts of London, the UK and Europe.

The Olympic Park is on a previously undeveloped site, easily accessible from central London.

The Olympic Park in the Lower Lea Valley will be a model of sustainable development.

Most of the Olympic venues are in London – concentrated at the Olympic Park and River Zone.

The Games will help to regenerate east London, one of the most deprived parts of the capital.

Now, put together your Games bid for your city. This is what your bid should contain:
- A poster to support your city's bid for the Olympic Games (page 87)
- A map to show the site of the Olympic Park in your city (page 90)
- A map to show the Olympic venues in and around your city (page 92–93)
- A map to show your city's transport links and the improvements you would make (page 94–95)
- A statement (up to 200 words) to explain how your bid would be sustainable (page 96–97)
- A statement (up to 200 words) to explain how the Olympic Games would regenerate your city and reduce deprivation (page 98–99).

6 Israel/Palestine – a land divided

Is building a barrier the best way to create peace?

KEY CONCEPTS
- Space
- Place
- Cultural understanding and diversity

coming up...

Two into one doesn't go, or so they say. In a small, crowded corner of the Middle East two peoples – Israelis and Palestinians – both claim the same TERRITORY. Palestinian terrorists kill Israelis with suicide bombs and Israel retaliates by firing missiles into Palestinian towns. Now, Israel has built a huge wall to protect itself.

through the unit...

You will explore the geography of Israel/Palestine to help you to understand the conflict. You will look at life on both sides of the wall to find out what concerns Israelis and Palestinians.

your final task...

You will decide whether building a barrier is the best way to create peace, or if there is a better option. Is it possible to share the land, so that two into one does go?

102 The wall separating Israeli and Palestinian territory

starter...

1 Read the story on the opposite page, or listen to it.
   a) As you read or listen, list all the places and events that are mentioned.
   b) Draw a map to tell the story, showing the places and events that are mentioned. Label the places and events on the map and give the map a title. Don't worry about how accurate your map is. You are drawing it to tell the story.

discuss...

2 a) Who do you think was to blame for what happened in the story? You can blame one, or more, of these people:
   - the three boys
   - their parents
   - the school
   - settlers in Netzarim
   - Israeli soldiers
   - groups like Hamas
   - the Israeli government.

   Give your reasons.

   b) What could any of these people have done differently to help to avoid the tragedy?

IS BUILDING A BARRIER THE BEST WAY TO CREATE PEACE?

April, 2002

It was the end of the school day at Salala Edeen school in Gaza City, the main city in the small Palestinian territory of Gaza. Three friends packed their school bags like the end of any normal school day. The friends (Youssef Zaqout, Anwar Hamdouna and Ismail Abu Nadi) were all fourteen. In their bags, hidden beneath the exercise books and pencil cases, they carried knives, an axe and home-made bombs. No one knew about their plan – not even their classmates.

As the school bell rang, they set off on a six-kilometre walk to the small, isolated Israeli SETTLEMENT of Netzarim. It was like many others dotted around Gaza. Altogether, there were about 6000 Israeli SETTLERS living in Gaza, among over one million Palestinians, protected by 10,000 Israeli soldiers.

Palestinian children have learned to hate the Israelis. In general, the only contact they have with them is with the Israeli soldiers who patrol the streets of Gaza. Over the years, many Palestinian children have been shot while throwing stones at tanks or the soldiers. Very few ever get near an Israeli settlement.

Later that evening, after their long walk, Youssef, Anwar and Ismail crawled through the dark towards Netzarim. But that was as close as they got. Within a few metres of the security fence that protected the settlement, Israeli soldiers shot them dead. Their bodies, riddled with bullets, were later returned to their distraught parents who also knew nothing of their plan.

All three had left notes to their families to say that they wanted to be 'martyrs'. They knew that their mission was doomed from the start. Youssef wrote, 'Oh mother, please be happy with me. I am giving my soul for the sake of God and the homeland. Don't cry for me. Bury me with my brothers, the martyrs.'

Anwar wrote, 'Dad, mum, forgive me. I am going to carry out a martyrdom operation against a settlement.' Ismail's friend, Mohammed, who sat next to him in class said, 'I had no idea he would do something like this. He was my friend. He used to say he wanted to be a doctor when he grew up, but now he's dead.'

All three boys were successful students from ordinary families. Where did their plan come from? Palestinians in Gaza, and other territory occupied by the Israeli army, feel powerless. Some have become so angry that they resort to terrorism. They join militant groups (like Hamas and Islamic Jihad) who carry out attacks against Israel. Although children are told not to take part in suicide attacks, some have tried to copy.

At the boys' funeral thousands of Palestinians marched behind their coffins to the cemetery in Gaza City. One teenager who was there said, 'It was a heroic act. Everybody wants to do it.'

In 2005, Israel evacuated its settlements in Gaza and withdrew its army. However, Israel still occupies much of the West Bank, a much larger Palestinian territory. In 2006, Hamas was elected to form the Palestinian government. In December 2008 Israel invaded Gaza to stop Palestinian rocket attacks. Over 1000 Palestinians died.

ISRAEL/PALESTINE – A LAND DIVIDED

➔ How the land is divided

To understand why Youssef, Anwar and Ismail risked their lives trying to bomb an Israeli settlement, you need to go back into history.

The modern STATE of Israel (map **A**) was founded in 1948 after the Second World War. It was claimed by the Jewish people as a new homeland, after six million Jews were killed by the Nazis during the war. However, it was not empty land – 700,000 Palestinian Arabs lived there. When the Israeli army arrived, Palestinians were forced to flee as REFUGEES.

From the start, Israel was in conflict with the Palestinians and with their other Arab neighbours (Egypt, Jordan, Syria and Lebanon). They refused to accept Israel's right to exist and wanted the refugees to be allowed to return. They even threatened to destroy Israel.

In 1967, Israel launched an attack on the countries around it. They occupied the territory around their BORDER in order to increase their security. They have since withdrawn from Sinai and Gaza, but they still occupy the West Bank and Golan Heights (map **B**). The West Bank is now home to nearly half a million Jewish settlers. The historic city of Jerusalem is divided between Jews and Palestinians.

Haram al Sharif in Jerusalem (a holy place for Muslim Palestinians)

The Wailing Wall in Jerusalem (a holy place for Jews)

A Israel and neighbouring countries today

IS BUILDING A BARRIER THE BEST WAY TO CREATE PEACE?

	Israel	Palestinian territories
Population	6.7 million	3.8 million
Area	22,072 km²	6,335 km²
Life expectancy	77 (men) 82 (women)	71 (men) 74 (women)
GDP/capita	$17,380	$1,120

Sources: UN and World Bank

C Israel and Palestinian territories compared

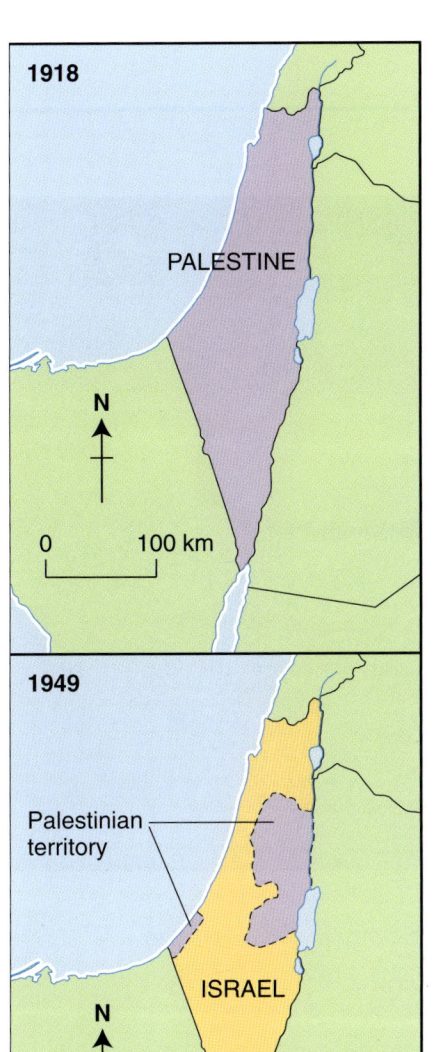

activity...

1. Look at the maps in **A** and **B**. How have the borders of Palestine and Israel changed since 1918? Write three sentences to describe who gained land and who lost land:
   a) from 1918 to 1949   b) from 1949 to 1967
   c) from 1967 to the present day.
2. Look at table **C** to compare Israel and the Palestinian territories now.
   a) Which area is most crowded? Explain how you can tell.
   b) Which area has the best quality of life? Explain how you can tell.

your concerns...

Work with a partner. Through the unit, one of you will be an Israeli and one will be a Palestinian.

1. Study the information on this spread and read what happened to you and your family below:
   - **the Israeli** Until 1942, your family were Jews living in Poland. Many of them died in the Nazi concentration camps in the Second World War. Some escaped to Israel and now you live in the wealthy city of Tel Aviv.
   - **the Palestinian** Until 1949, your family lived in Palestine. When Israel took the land, they were forced to leave and flee to a refugee camp in Jordan. You are still living there today.
2. What are your main concerns about the future, based on what you have learnt so far?
   For example, as an Israeli, you could be concerned that neighbouring countries still want to attack you. As a Palestinian, you could be concerned that you are a refugee with no permanent home. Write your concerns down. Keep your list and add to it through the unit.

B Changing borders in the Middle East

ISRAEL/PALESTINE – A LAND DIVIDED

➡ People without a home

Before the state of Israel was created in 1948, Palestine was a quiet corner of the Middle East inhabited by a majority of Palestinians living peacefully with their Jewish neighbours. This passage describes an idyllic childhood in Palestine in the 1940s.

I shinnied higher up the fig tree – up to the very top, where the branches bent at dangerous angles under my weight. This was my special place.

Now, with one arm crooked around the topmost branch, I pushed aside the curled leaves, thrusting my head out into the spring sun which was slanting towards late afternoon. Row after row of fig trees spread for several acres, stretching down the hill away from our house, covering the slope with rustling greenery. The broadening leaves concealed a fresh-water spring and a dark mossy grotto where our goats and cattle sheltered themselves in summer. Beyond our orchards rose the lush, majestic highlands of upper Galilee. They looked purple in the distance – 'the most beautiful land in all of Palestine,' father said so often. A dreamy look would mist into his pale blue eyes then, as it did whenever he spoke about his beloved land.

With a recklessness that would pale my mother, I swung down from the treetop and flung myself to the ground. Then I was off, running toward the centre of the village.

I darted through the narrow streets – hardly streets at all, but foot-worn, dirt corridors that threaded the homes of the village together beneath the shade of cedar and silver-green olive trees – dodging a goat and some chickens in my path. Biram (the village's name) seemed like one huge house to me. Our family, the Chacours, had led their flocks to these, the highest hills of Galilee, many hundreds of years ago. My grandparents had always lived here, nearly next door to us. And there were so many aunts, uncles, cousins and distant relatives clustered here, it was as if each stone dwelling was merely another room where another bit of my family lived. Biram had grown here, quietly rearing its children, reaping its harvests, dozing beneath the Mediterranean stars for so many generations that all households were as one family.

Extract from *Blood Brothers*, by Elias Chacour

Soon after this incident, in 1948, Israeli soldiers came to Biram. Families were told to leave the village and later their homes destroyed. Upper Galilee became part of the new state of Israel. The people of Biram joined the flood of refugees who left Palestine and who have never returned.

106

IS BUILDING A BARRIER THE BEST WAY TO CREATE PEACE?

Today, there are almost four million Palestinian refugees scattered around the Middle East and North Africa, as you can see in map **D**.

D Where Palestinian refugees live today

Source: Atlas of War and Peace

activity...

1 Read Elias Chacour's account of his childhood in Biram, or listen to it.
   a) List the adjectives used in the story to describe the landscape, for example, lush, majestic. Try to picture the view from the treetop, of the village and its surroundings.
   b) Draw the view you can see.
2 Look at photo **E**, showing a Palestinian refugee camp.
   a) List as many adjectives as you can to describe the view in this photo.
   b) Write an account of life in a refugee camp, using your own adjectives. Like Elias' account of Biram, you could imagine yourself watching from somewhere in the photo to describe what you see.

E Palestinian REFUGEE CAMP in Jordan

aim high...

3 Look at map **D**.
   a) Describe the distribution of Palestinian refugees shown on the map.
   b) How can you explain the pattern?

your concerns...

You are a Palestinian or an Israeli. Study the information on this spread. What are your concerns about the future, based on what you have learnt? Add them to the list you started.

ISRAEL/PALESTINE – A LAND DIVIDED

➡ The promised land

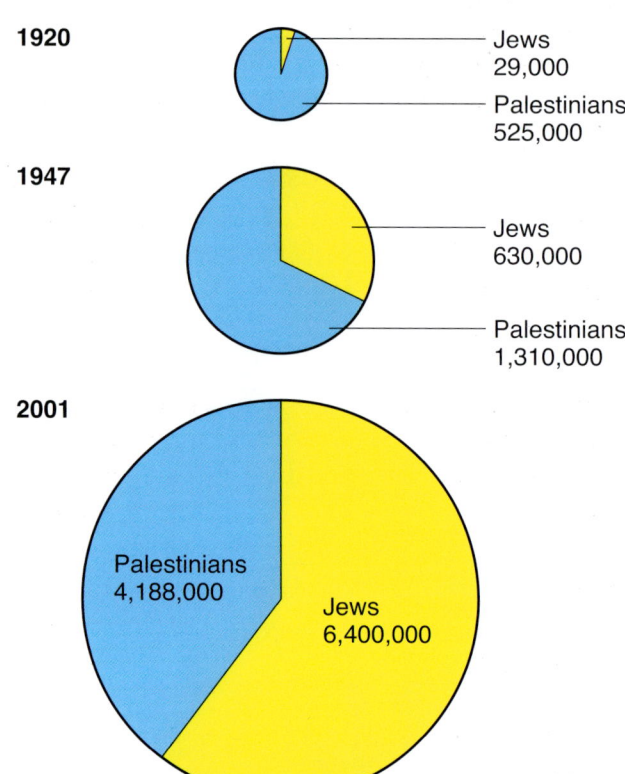

1920
- Jews 29,000
- Palestinians 525,000

1947
- Jews 630,000
- Palestinians 1,310,000

2001
- Palestinians 4,188,000
- Jews 6,400,000

Many Jews believe that Israel is the land promised to them by God in the Bible. Since the early twentieth century, they have been returning to their ancestral home in the Middle East to escape persecution in other parts of the world. Their numbers increased dramatically at the end of the Second World War and have continued growing. Today, Jews outnumber Palestinians (source **F**).

Since the war in 1967, hundreds of new Israeli settlements have been built in the occupied West Bank – land that belongs to Palestinians. Many of the settlements (like Elon Moreh opposite) are cut off from the rest of Israel and need to be defended against Palestinian attacks.

F Population growth in Palestine/Israel

Beautiful mountain views and clear air – many Israelis believe this is the 'Promised Land'

Modern highways, built through Palestinian land, link the settlements with the rest of Israel

Settlements are built on hilltops overlooking Palestinian towns and villages

Settlers receive government loans to encourage them to buy homes here

Architect-designed homes and lush, green lawns depend on scarce water

Surrounded by barbed-wire and electric fences, settlements are defended from possible attack

G A new Israeli settlement in the West Bank

IS BUILDING A BARRIER THE BEST WAY TO CREATE PEACE?

'When, as a new immigrant, I arrived in Israel 33 years ago, my wife and I, with our two children, joined a group of families that decided to settle in Samaria. There were no Jewish families living in Samaria at the time and, because of its importance as the place where the Jewish nation began, we chose the area of Elon Moreh.

The Bible first mentions Elon Moreh when God tells Abram to leave his father's home and go to the land He will show him. 'And Abram passed through the land unto the place of Shechem, unto the oak (Hebrew: elon) of Moreh.' (Genesis 12:6) Here, God tells Abram 'to your children I will give this land'.

In 1980, our community moved to the site of the present village on a mountaintop overlooking the city of Shechem (the Palestinian city of Nablus). Today, 250 families from 25 countries live here, over twenty per cent recent immigrants from Peru, Russia, India, the US and England.

Elon Moreh has a large mini-market, stores selling books and stationery, clothing stores, and offers a variety of services, from barbers to electricians, plumbers to gardeners. There is a swimming pool, sports centre with gymnasium and exercise room. Medical services include a hospital and dental clinic. Education is a high priority in this religious community, providing mixed religious and military training. Over the years, Elon Moreh has suffered more than its share from Arab terror. The worst single disaster occurred during the Passover of 2002, when a terrorist shot his way into the home of Rabbi David Gavish. The terrorist killed David, his wife Rachel, their oldest son Abraham and Rachel's father, Yitzhak Kaner.

The murder of the Gavish family was a tremendous shock and we feared many families would leave. In fact, not a single family left in response to the tragedy and many new families have continued to come. We have built a security perimeter around Elon Moreh, and special cameras and monitors ensure this kind of tragedy will not happen again.

Today, the homes of tens of thousands of Jews, with their schools, factories, vineyards and orchards, cover the hills of Samaria. Our supporters abroad, especially American Friends of Elon Moreh, give families here the sense they are not alone in their struggle to build and grow in this biblical homeland of the Jewish people.'

Zeev Saffer, a resident of Elon Moreh

Source: Mideast Outpost

activity...

1 Look at the pie charts in **F**. You are going to turn them into a multiple line graph.
   a) Draw two large axes.
   b) Draw two lines to show the growth of Jewish and Palestinian populations, using the data on the pie charts. Label the two lines.
   c) What does the graph show you about changes in the two populations?
2 Look at photo **G** and read Zeev Saffer's story.
   a) Give three positive and three negative aspects of life in a settlement in the West Bank.
   b) One factor, above all others, inspired Jews to build their settlements here and to stay. What is it?

aim high...

3 a) Why are the Israeli settlements built on mountaintops, do you think? Give a reason.
   b) What would be the problems with this location? Think of at least three.

your concerns...

You are a Palestinian or an Israeli. Study the information on this spread. What are your concerns about the future, based on what you have learnt. Add them to your list.

ISRAEL/PALESTINE – A LAND DIVIDED

→ Scarce water

Population growth puts pressure on resources – especially water. The Middle East has a dry climate, so water is always in short supply. Today, with over ten million people, there is a water crisis. Israel no longer has enough water for its cities and farms. The situation for Palestinians is even worse. Each Palestinian uses only one fifth of the water used by an Israeli (source **H**).

Israel controls most of the water supply. In map **J**, the River Jordan flows north to south between Jordan and the West Bank. Israel extracts 75 per cent of the river's water, carrying it by canal and pipe to the driest coastal areas. Similarly, it extracts underground water from the mountain AQUIFER beneath the West Bank, so lowering the WATER TABLE and depriving Palestinians of vital water (cross-section **I**).

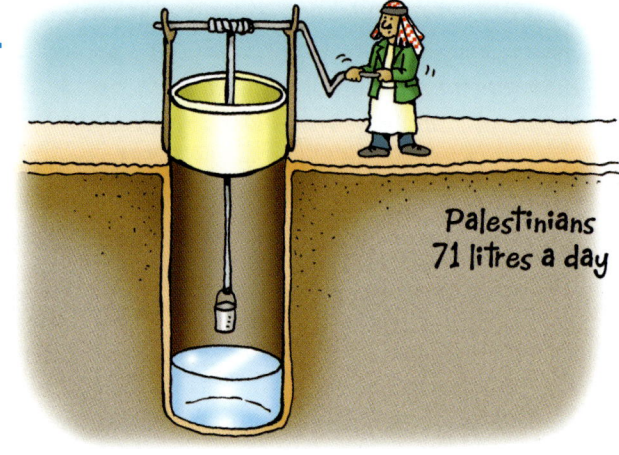

Palestinians 71 litres a day

Israelis 350 litres a day

H The average daily amount of water used per person

I Water sources

The coastal plain is where most of Israel's population live. Water is used in cities and for farming. It is piped from the River Jordan and from the aquifer beneath the West Bank.

ISRAEL

MEDITERRANEAN SEA

GROUNDWATER in the coastal aquifer is polluted by seawater as the water table gets lower. In future, Israel could obtain water by **DESALINATING** seawater.

IS BUILDING A BARRIER THE BEST WAY TO CREATE PEACE?

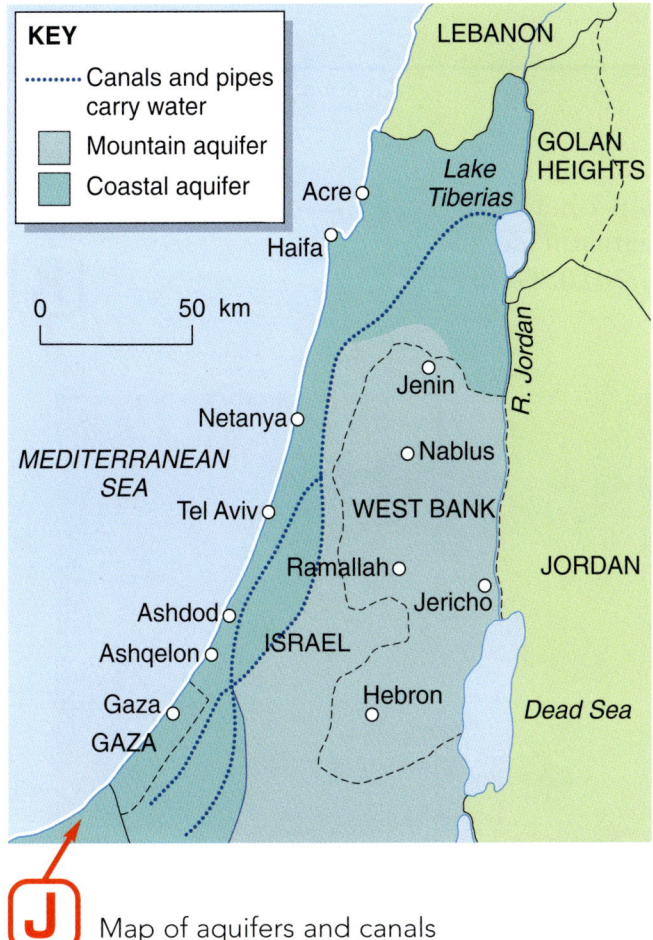

J Map of aquifers and canals

activity...

1. Compare the amount of water used by some everyday domestic activities with the amounts in graph **H**.
   - flushing the toilet: six litres
   - running the tap: six litres per minute
   - washing up: ten litres
   - taking a shower: seven litres per minute
   - taking a bath: 80 litres
   - using a washing machine: 50 litres.

   Suggest how a typical person would use their daily water supply if they were:
   a) a Palestinian living in the West Bank
   b) an Israeli living in Tel Aviv.

2. Compare cross-section **I** with map **J**. Find Nabulus and Tel Aviv on the map. For each city:
   a) Where does it obtain its water from?
   b) What water supply problems does it have?
   c) Which is most likely to have a reliable water supply? Why?

your concerns...

You are a Palestinian or an Israeli. Study the information on this spread. What are your concerns about the future, based on what you have learnt. Add them to your list.

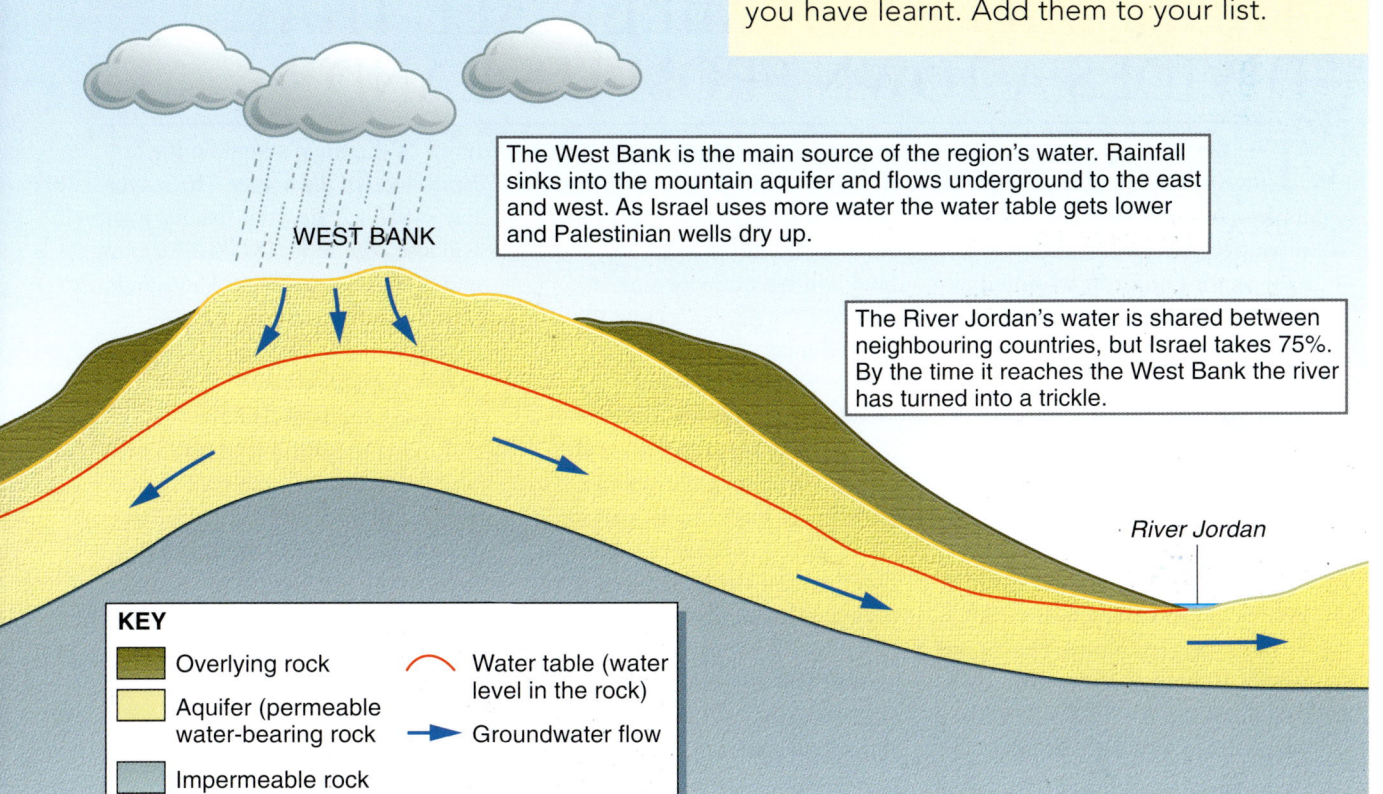

ISRAEL/PALESTINE – A LAND DIVIDED

Living with the wall

In 2002, the Israeli government started to build an eight metre high wall to surround the West Bank (map **L**). They believe the barrier will bring an end to Palestinian suicide bombings in Israel. It will not be complete until 2010. Gaza already has a similar barrier.

THE £1 MILLION-A-MILE WALL THAT DIVIDES A TOWN FROM ITS LAND
26 November 2002

The first that the people of Jayyous knew of the wall was a piece of paper flapping from an olive tree. "It was a military order," said Sharif Omar. "It informed us we had to meet an Israeli army officer the next weekend and follow him to see the route of the wall. We were shocked, very shocked when we saw where it was going. People just burst into tears. Some fainted."

That was in September. Since then the bulldozers have cleared a swathe of land 50 metres wide through Jayyous's olive groves and within 10 metres of the town. In a few more weeks, the concrete foundations of a wall 8m high will be in place. A trench, barbed wire, floodlights, cameras and electronic detectors will follow. The wall, severing the town from much of its land will become one link in a concrete barrier encircling the West Bank.

The Israeli government is spending £1 million a mile to build this massive fortification, in the belief it will keep the suicide bombers at bay. Israelis call it the terror wall. Palestinians say it will turn the West Bank into the world's biggest prison.

In Jayyous they are worried, not so much about being shut in as shut out. The wall wriggles its way through the heart of Jayyous leaving more of the town's land on the Israeli side of the border. The mayor, Fayez Salim, calculates that the town will lose 80% of its 18,000 olive trees and 50,000 citrus trees. Thousands of jobs will be lost during the annual harvest. Crucially, Jayyous will be separated from its seven wells and the Israelis have forbidden the drilling of new ones.

Palestinians say the wall serves a dual purpose – to cage together West Bank residents behind security fences and to seize yet more land by allowing the expansion of Jewish settlements between the 1967 border and the wall.

Extract adapted from the *Guardian* newspaper

IS BUILDING A BARRIER THE BEST WAY TO CREATE PEACE?

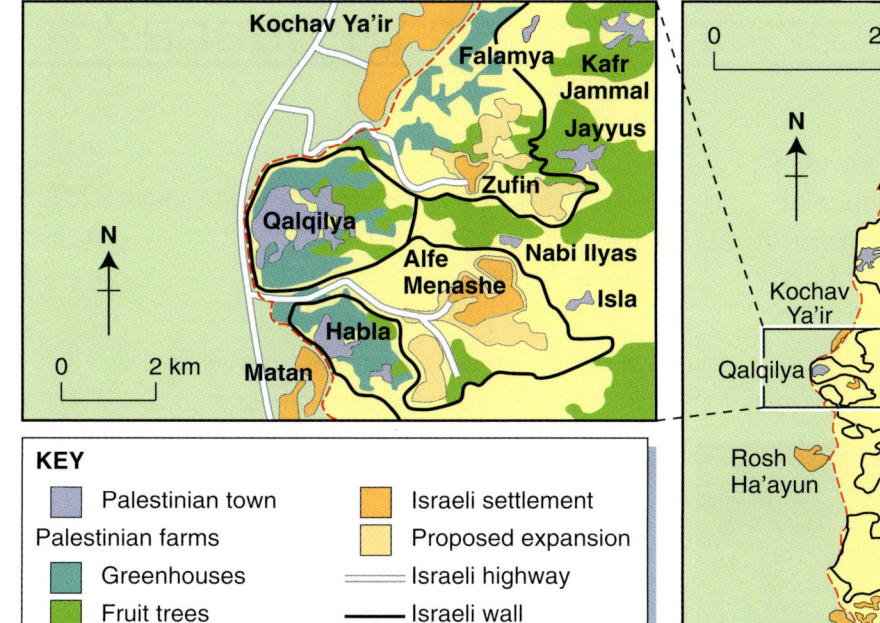

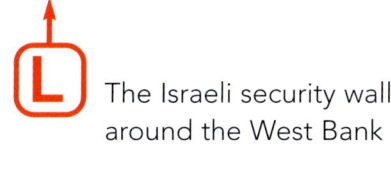

L The Israeli security wall around the West Bank

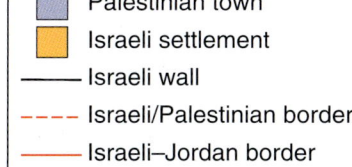

activity...

1 Read newspaper extract **K**. What is the purpose of the wall:
   a) according to the Israeli view?
   b) according to the Palestinian view?

aim high...

2 Look carefully at map **L**.
   What evidence can you find on the map to support either the Israeli or Palestinian view about what the wall is for? Write a paragraph to explain.

discuss...

3 a) Why are Palestinians against the wall? How are they likely to respond?
   b) Most Israelis are in favour of the wall because they feel safer. Are they right to feel safer? Why, or why not?

your concerns...

You are a Palestinian or an Israeli. Study the information on this spread. What are your concerns about the future, based on what you have learnt. Add them to your list.

ISRAEL/PALESTINE – A LAND DIVIDED

A barrier to terrorists – or to peace?

Since Israel has started to build the wall there has been a drop in the number of Palestinian terrorist attacks. However, not all Israelis are confident that the new barrier will put an end to suicide bombings. One Israeli, with firsthand experience of terrorism, explains why.

> My name is Rami Elhanan. On 4 September 1997, I lost my 14-year-old daughter, Smadar, in a suicide attack on Ben Yahuda Street in Jerusalem.
>
> When the first suicide bombs went off, Israelis could not understand how someone could kill himself and little kids. There was no explanation. From this fear came anger, and from the anger came a very strong public demand for a barrier to hide behind…
>
> But for myself, personally, I don't believe in walls. I don't think barriers create good neighbours. Barriers create hate, especially if you build it in the middle of your neighbour's living room instead of your own backyard.

Extract from *Barrier to peace?* CSM and World Vision

 Graffiti on the Israeli wall

activity…

1. Look at photo **M**.
   a) What do you think the message of the graffiti is?
   b) Which side of the wall is it on? Give reasons for your answer.
2. Read Rami Elhanan's opinion.
   a) Do you think it is an opinion most Israelis would share? Explain your answer.
   b) Do you agree with him? Give your reasons.

■ your final task…

Over the years, there have been peace agreements between Israel and the Palestinians. But none of them have lasted. The problem lies in the detail. Every bit of land and drop of water is precious, so no one wants to give up what they have got. Peace agreements are no use if they don't work on the ground.

You are going to work with a partner to make a peace agreement in one imaginary area on the border between Israel and the West Bank. At the end you will produce a joint plan for the area.

One of you will represent the Israeli side and the other will represent the Palestinian side. First, on your own:

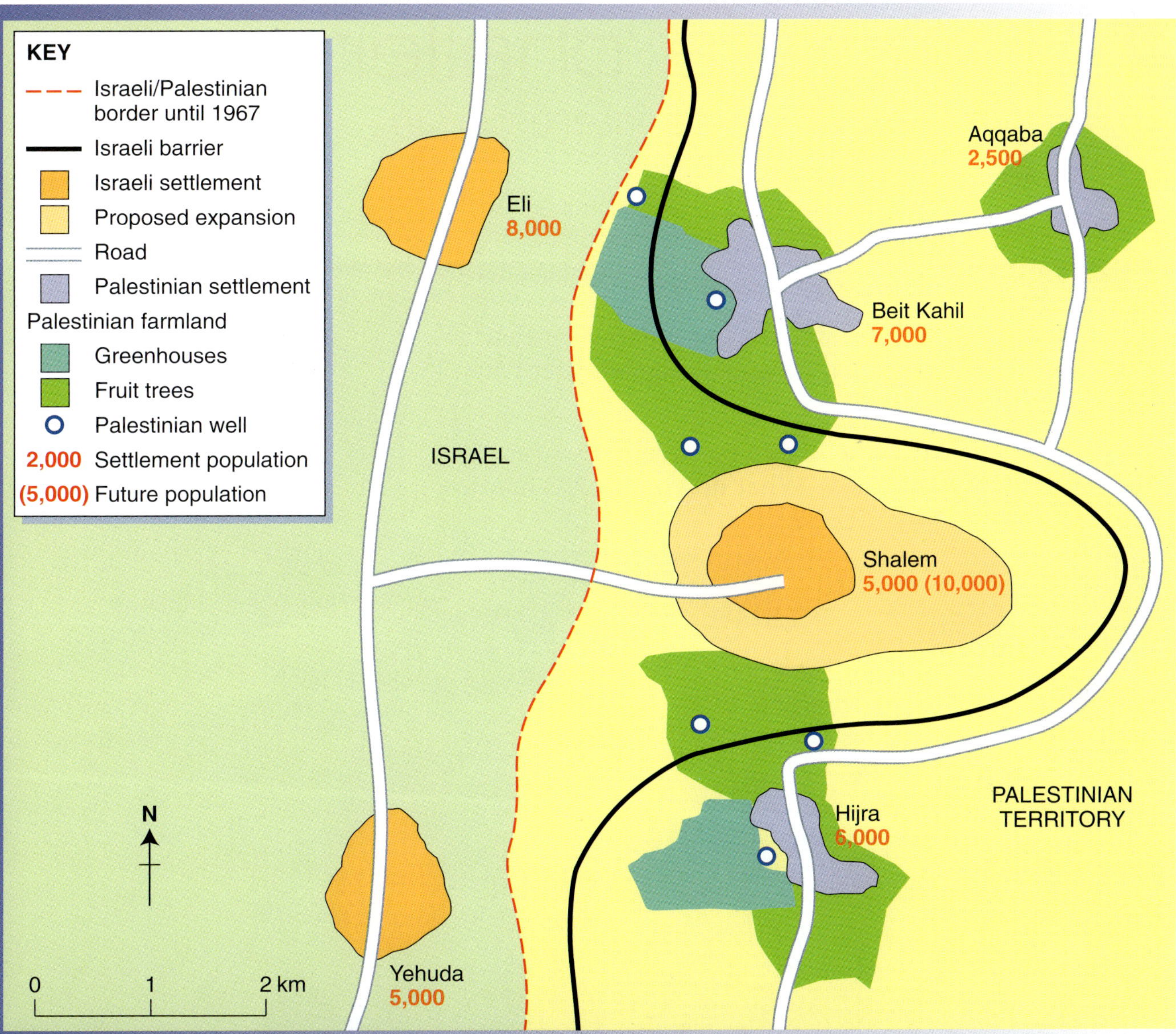

IS BUILDING A BARRIER THE BEST WAY TO CREATE PEACE?

Map of imaginary section of Israeli wall, separating Israel from West Bank

1 Study the map of the area.
2 Read the list of concerns you have written through the unit. How would you change the map to meet your concerns?
3 Redraw the map to plan how you would like the area to be. You need to think about four questions:
   - should the barrier stay where it is or should it be demolished?
   - if it is demolished, should it be rebuilt elsewhere?
   - should Israeli settlements on Palestinian land be expanded or removed?
   - how should land and resources be shared?

Then, together with your partner:
4 Share your plan with your partner. Look at their plan. Now comes the difficult bit! You have to produce a joint plan that you can both agree on. This could mean that you have to make compromises – agree to some changes that you don't want, to get some that you do.
5 Draw your final plan. Write two paragraphs to explain how the plan helps to meet the concerns of Israelis and Palestinians.

7 Antarctica – the ultimate challenge

Why should we be interested in Antarctica?

KEY CONCEPT

- **Place**
- Physical processes
- Environmental interaction + sustainable development

This is Antarctica. It's the world's last great WILDERNESS – a vast, uninhabited continent, almost completely covered in snow and ice.

Imagine what it would be like to be here. As you unzip the tent and look outside… What do you see? What do you hear? What do you feel?

WHY SHOULD WE BE INTERESTED IN ANTARCTICA?

coming up...
Increasingly, people are interested in Antarctica: scientists, environmentalists, governments and even tourists. The question is, why are they interested in such a cold, remote, dangerous place?

through the unit...
You will plan an expedition to Antarctica. You will identify the challenges you might face and think of questions to investigate.

your final task...
You will make a proposal for a new expedition to Antarctica. The challenge is to come up with such a good proposal that a sponsor would pay for the expedition.

starter...
1 a) What do you already know about Antarctica? Draw a large spider diagram like this to show your ideas.

You can add more ideas as you go through the unit.

b) What more would you like to know about Antarctica? Write down at least five questions.

2 Suggest what each of these would find interesting in Antarctica:
   a) a scientist
   b) an environmentalist
   c) a government
   d) a tourist.

your expedition...
You are planning an expedition to Antarctica. As you go through the unit,
1 Make a note of the challenges you could face on your expedition. For example, *Antarctica is a long way from anywhere*. Think of how you would overcome the challenges. For example, *go by boat or plane*.
2 Think of geographical questions you could investigate. For example, *How do penguins survive here?* Suggest how you would investigate your question.

At the end of the unit, you will put together your ideas to make a proposal for an expedition to Antarctica. You will list all the items you need for your expedition and choose the best question to investigate.

ANTARCTICA – THE ULTIMATE CHALLENGE

→ The white continent

Here is a map of Antarctica. It is centred on the SOUTH POLE, so south is in the middle and north is in every direction going towards the edge of the map.

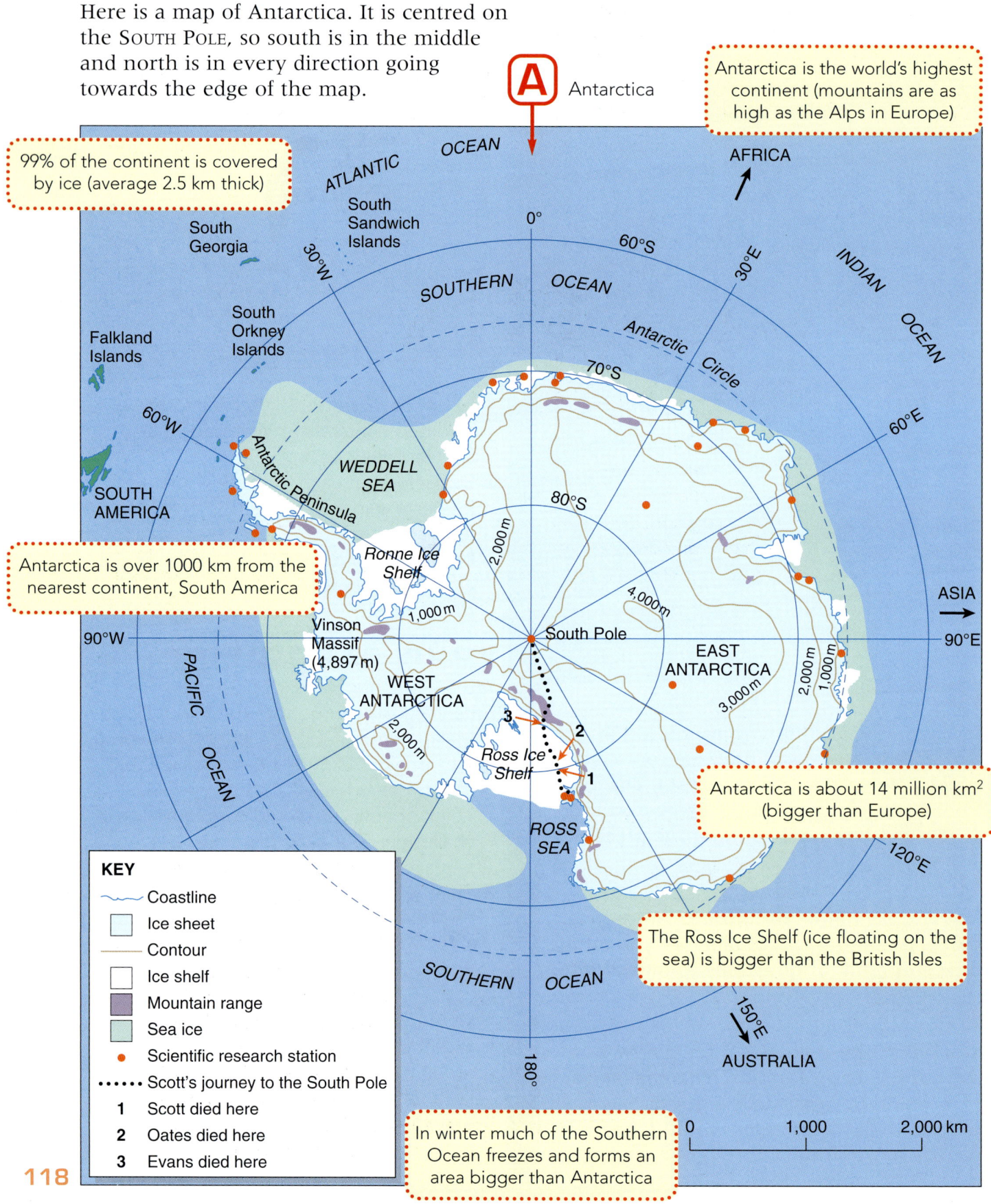

WHY SHOULD WE BE INTERESTED IN ANTARCTICA?

The story of Scott's expedition to the South Pole

Nearly 100 years ago, an ill-fated British expedition led by Captain Robert Scott set out to become the first to reach the South Pole. The journey turned into a race when Scott discovered that a Norwegian, Roald Amundsen, was also leading an expedition to the Pole.

Sixteen men began the journey from the northern edge of the Ross Ice Shelf (map **A**) on 1 November 1911 using motor sledges, ponies and dogs to carry provisions. In the event, the motors broke down and the ponies died. For most of the journey the men had to pull their own provisions.

As they travelled to the Pole, they set up depots of provisions along the way for the return journey. At each depot some of the party turned back, leaving just five men to make the final leg of the journey to the South Pole. They reached the Pole on 17 January 1912 only to discover that Amundsen had arrived first on 14 December 1911. He had left a tent and a Norwegian flag.

However, that was not the only bad news. On the return journey the weather got worse. The men began to suffer from frostbite and malnutrition. One of them – Evans – collapsed and died. Another – Oates – was so badly affected, he decided to sacrifice himself so the others would make better progress. One evening he left the tent with the famous words, 'I am just going outside and may be some time.' He was never seen again.

Unfortunately, his sacrifice was in vain. A few days later, stuck in a blizzard, Scott and his two remaining companions died in their tent, frozen to death.

activity...

1. Look at map **A**.
   a) In which direction did Scott's expedition travel to the South Pole?
   b) How far did they travel there and back? Measure the distance using the scale.
   c) Roughly, how high did they climb? Look at the contour lines.
2. Study the map carefully.
   a) Where did the journey start? Be as accurate as you can.
   b) Why do you think they chose this point?
   c) Scott travelled to Antarctica by boat. Would he have been able to sail all the way to the starting point? Explain.

aim high...

3. Around Antarctica today there are many scientific research stations.
   a) Describe the distribution of these stations on the map. Write one or two sentences.
   b) Try to explain the distribution.
   c) Suggest why there are scientific research stations in Antarctica (you will find out more later).

your expedition...

1. What challenges could you face on your expedition? Think how you would overcome them. (There's no shortage of ideas in the story of Scott's expedition.)
2. What geographical question could you investigate? Suggest how you might investigate it. (It's early days, so don't worry if you can't think of any.)

ANTARCTICA – THE ULTIMATE CHALLENGE

→ It's perishing at the Pole!

The average temperature throughout the year at the South Pole is –50 °C. Even in summer, when the Sun shines 24 hours a day, the temperature stays below freezing. Though it is light all the time the angle of the Sun in the sky is low, so it doesn't give much heat (see **B**).

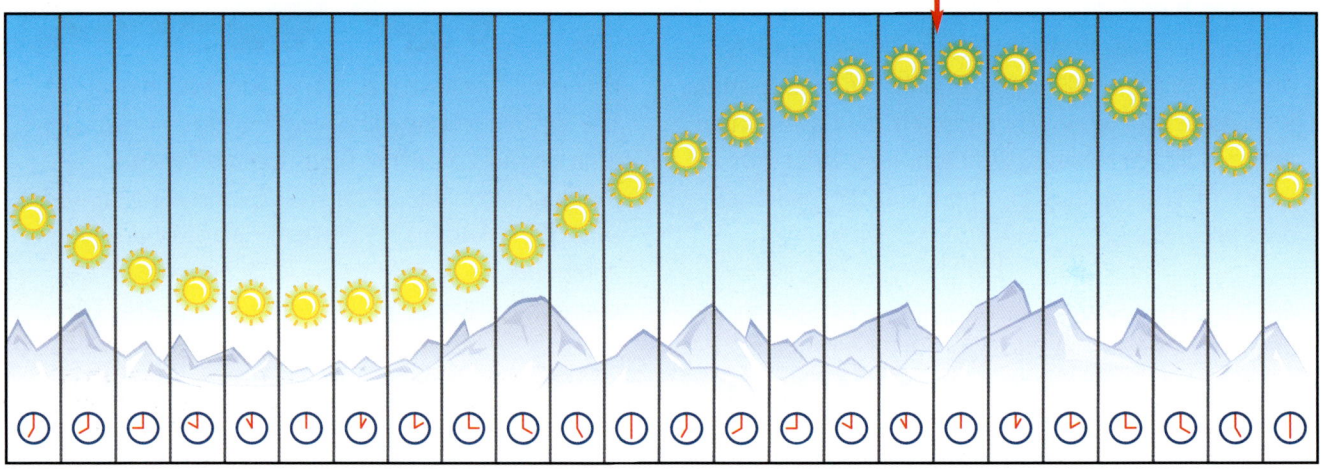

B The changing position of the Sun in the sky on a summer's day in Antarctica

It gets even colder in winter. The Sun disappears and there is darkness 24 hours a day. In Antarctica it is midsummer in December and midwinter in June (see **C**).

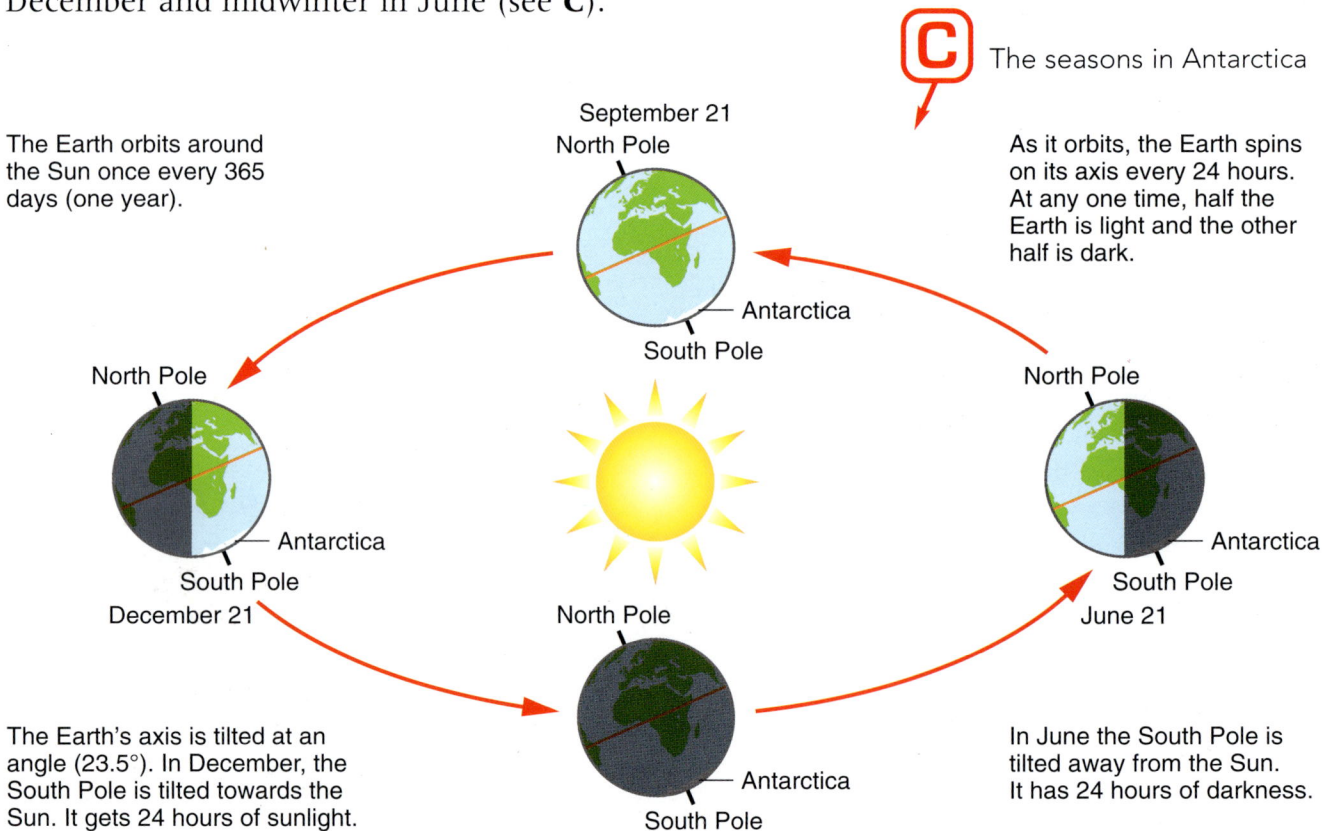

C The seasons in Antarctica

The Earth orbits around the Sun once every 365 days (one year).

As it orbits, the Earth spins on its axis every 24 hours. At any one time, half the Earth is light and the other half is dark.

The Earth's axis is tilted at an angle (23.5°). In December, the South Pole is tilted towards the Sun. It gets 24 hours of sunlight.

In June the South Pole is tilted away from the Sun. It has 24 hours of darkness.

WHY SHOULD WE BE INTERESTED IN ANTARCTICA?

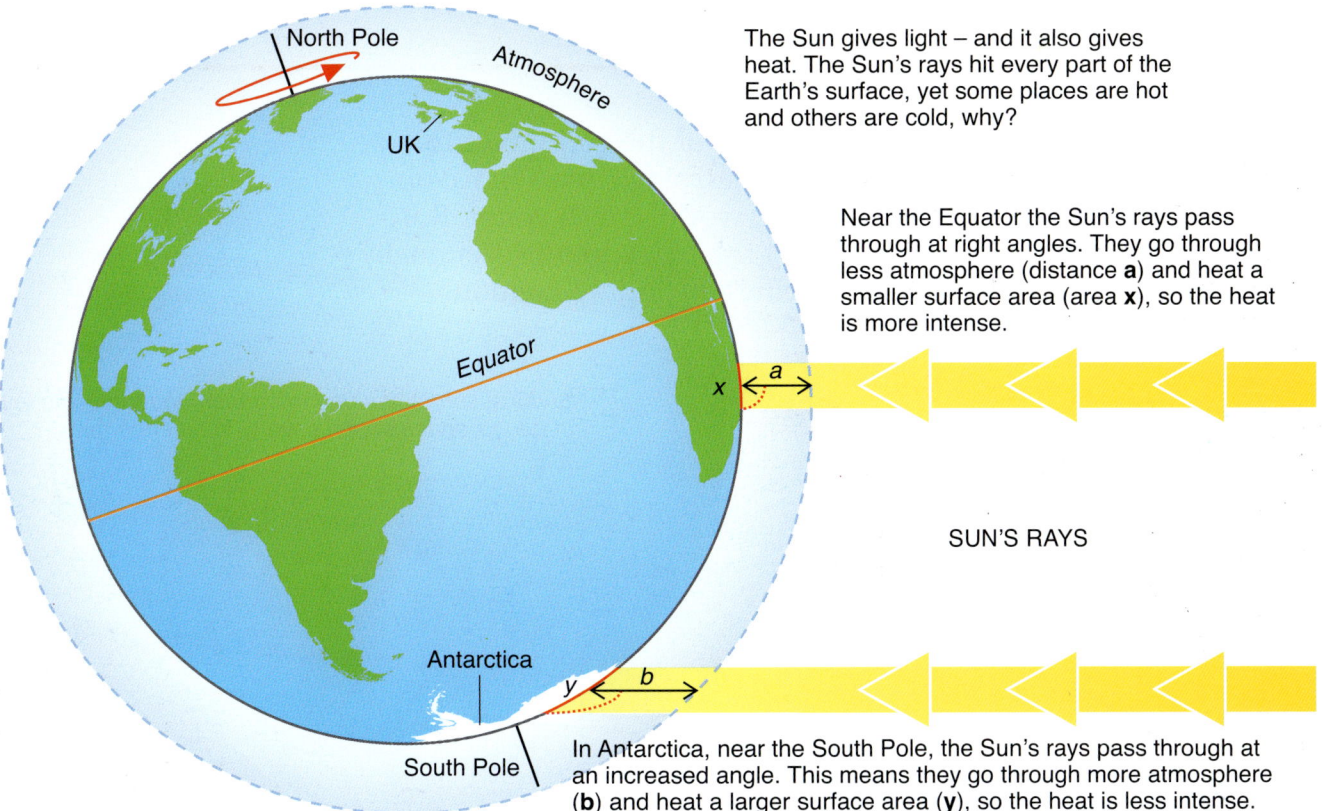

The Sun gives light – and it also gives heat. The Sun's rays hit every part of the Earth's surface, yet some places are hot and others are cold, why?

Near the Equator the Sun's rays pass through at right angles. They go through less atmosphere (distance **a**) and heat a smaller surface area (area **x**), so the heat is more intense.

SUN'S RAYS

In Antarctica, near the South Pole, the Sun's rays pass through at an increased angle. This means they go through more atmosphere (**b**) and heat a larger surface area (**y**), so the heat is less intense.

D The position of the Earth in December

activity...

1 Look at drawing **B**.
   a) Describe how the position of the Sun changes in the sky, over 24 hours in Antarctica on a summer's day.
   b) Which month of the year do you think this is? (Clue: look at drawing **C**)
2 Look at drawing **C**.
   a) Which time of year would be best for an expedition to Antarctica – June or December? Give two reasons.
   b) If you were going to the Arctic instead, when would you go? Explain why.
3 Look at drawing **D**.
   a) Why is Antarctica colder than the Equator? Complete this passage.
      In Antarctica, the Sun's rays travel through _____ atmosphere and heat a _____ surface area, so the heat is _____. In contrast, near the Equator…
   b) Now, explain why the Equator is hotter than the UK.

aim high...

4 You are given a torch and a sheet of paper. How could you use them to show why it is colder in Antarctica than it is at the Equator?

your expedition...

1 What challenges could you face on your expedition? Think how you would overcome them.
2 What geographical question could you investigate? Suggest how you might investigate it.

121

ANTARCTICA – THE ULTIMATE CHALLENGE

➜ On thick ice

The Antarctic ICE SHEET covers 99 per cent of the continent. In places it is nearly 5 km thick. It is the largest single mass of ice on Earth and it contains 90 per cent of the world's fresh water. If it were to melt, the world's oceans would rise by 70 metres – enough to flood many of the world's largest cities, including London.

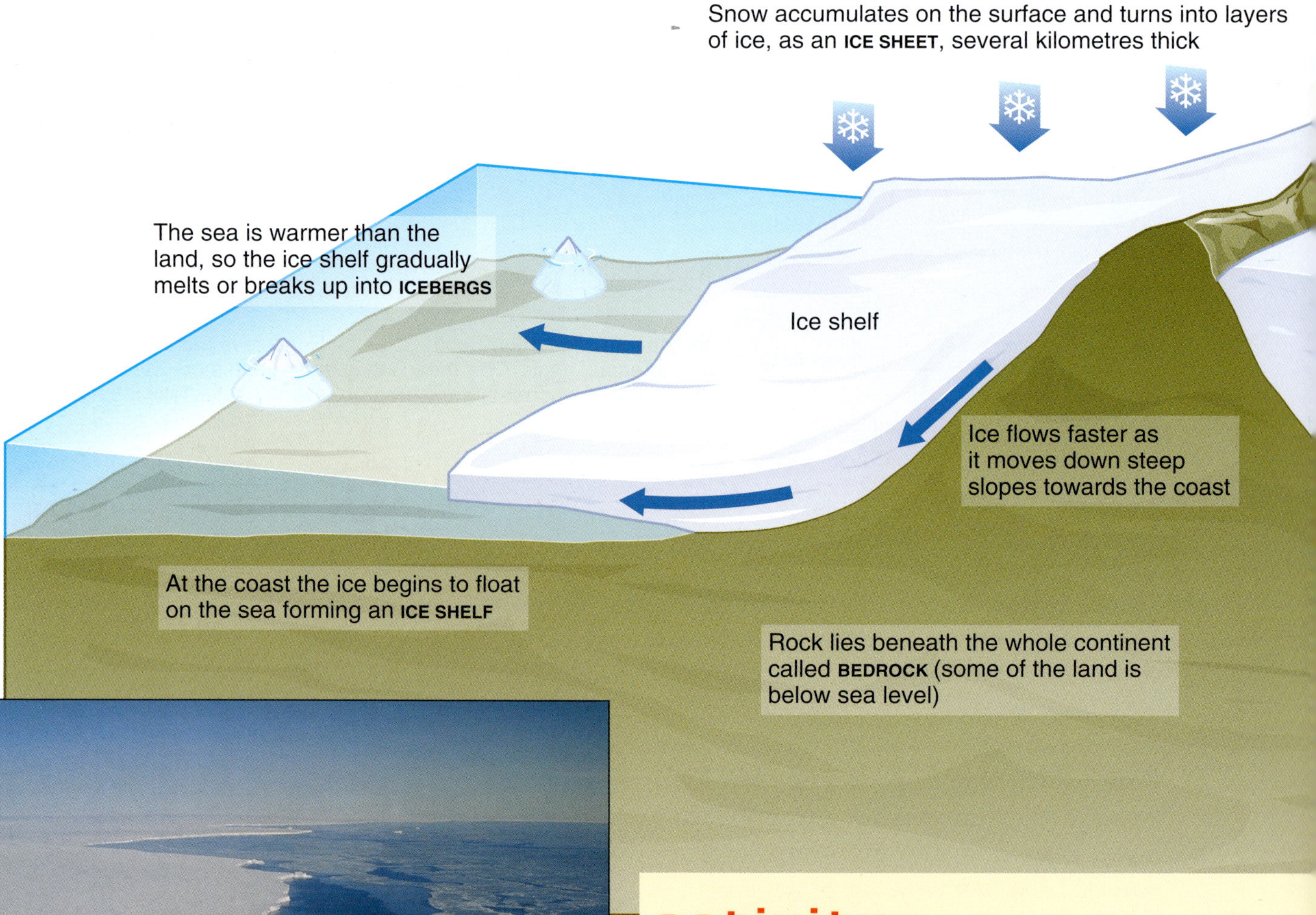

Snow accumulates on the surface and turns into layers of ice, as an **ICE SHEET**, several kilometres thick

The sea is warmer than the land, so the ice shelf gradually melts or breaks up into **ICEBERGS**

Ice shelf

Ice flows faster as it moves down steep slopes towards the coast

At the coast the ice begins to float on the sea forming an **ICE SHELF**

Rock lies beneath the whole continent called **BEDROCK** (some of the land is below sea level)

activity...

1. Look at cross-section **E**.
   a) Explain why Antarctica is a difficult environment to travel around. Give at least two reasons.
   b) Identify any particular hazards. Explain how they could be dangerous. (Clue: look at the photos.)
2. You are going to draw a simple flow diagram of an ice sheet.
   a) Draw a large copy of a cross-section like the one opposite.

WHY SHOULD WE BE INTERESTED IN ANTARCTICA?

E Cross-section of Antarctica

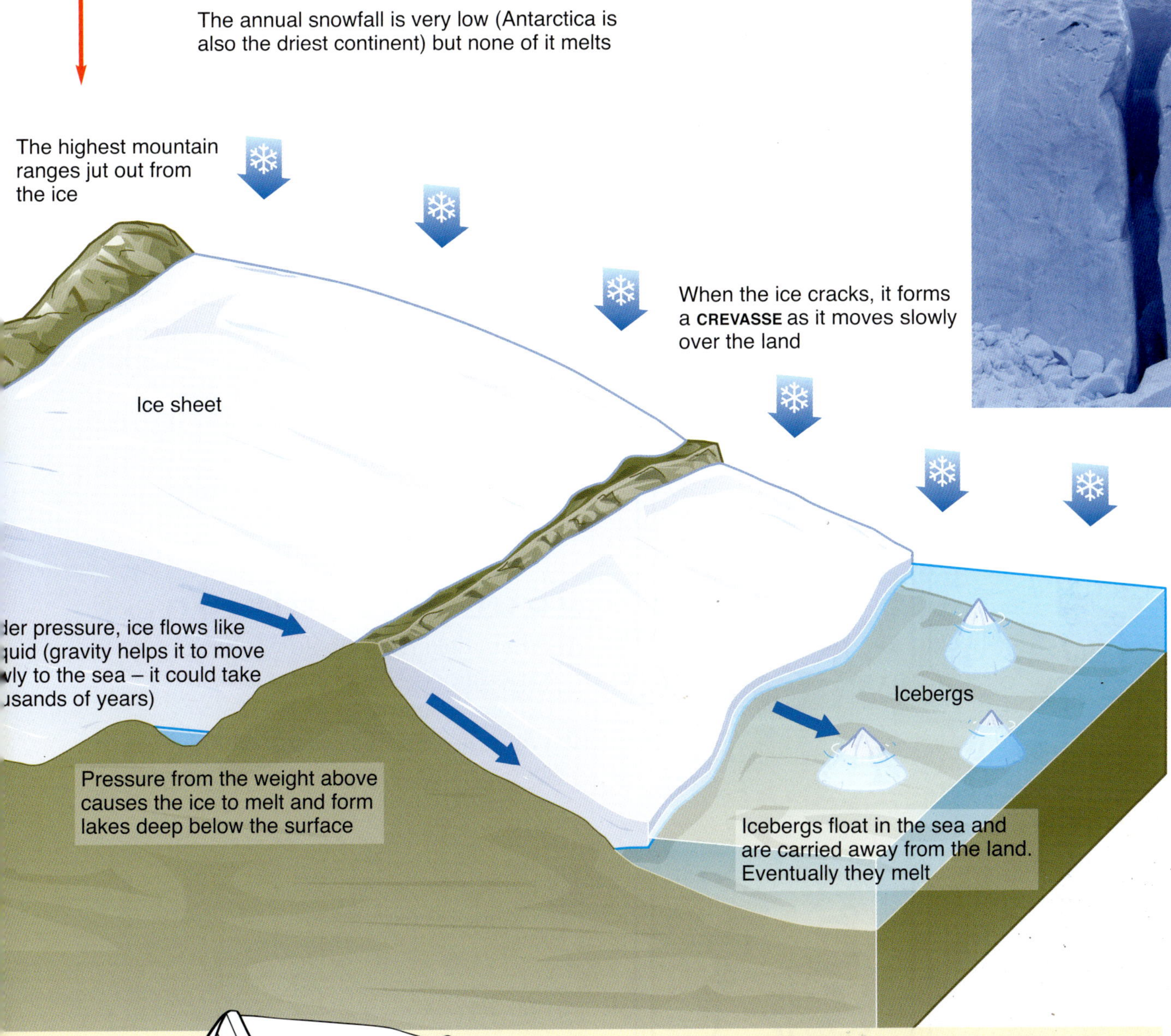

A CREVASSE

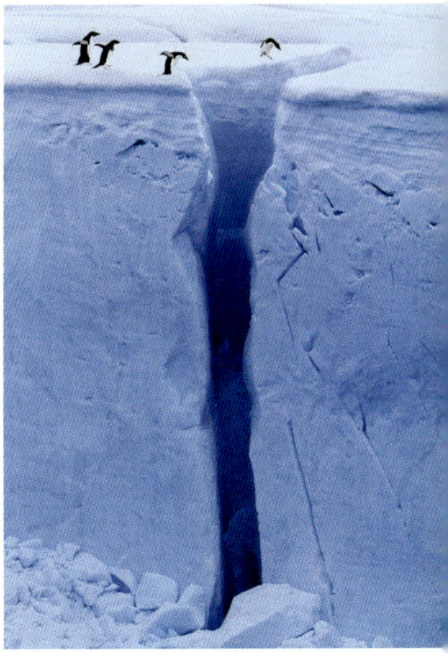

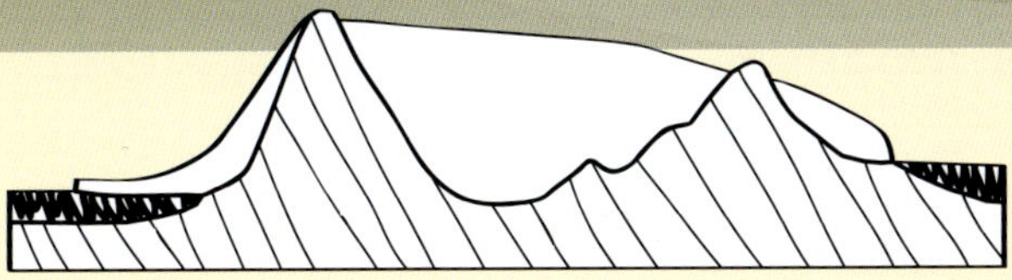

The annual snowfall is very low (Antarctica is also the driest continent) but none of it melts

The highest mountain ranges jut out from the ice

Ice sheet

When the ice cracks, it forms a **CREVASSE** as it moves slowly over the land

Under pressure, ice flows like liquid (gravity helps it to move slowly to the sea – it could take thousands of years)

Icebergs

Pressure from the weight above causes the ice to melt and form lakes deep below the surface

Icebergs float in the sea and are carried away from the land. Eventually they melt

b) Now, draw arrows on your diagram to show: **i)** snowfall **ii)** ice movement **iii)** melting. Label them.

your expedition...

1 What challenges could you face on your expedition? Think how you would overcome them.
2 What geographical question could you investigate? Suggest how you might investigate it.

aim high...

3 Predict the effects that you think global warming could have on different parts of Antarctica. (Think carefully. Don't just say the ice would melt!) You can find out later if your predictions are right.

ANTARCTICA – THE ULTIMATE CHALLENGE

→ Life in the deep freeze

The main challenge of living in Antarctica is the danger of getting too cold and dying from HYPOTHERMIA (source **F**). Some scientists do manage to live there. They work at RESEARCH STATIONS scattered around the continent. To survive, they need plenty of food, clothing, fuel and shelter. A few scientists brave the Antarctic winter every year.

activity...

1 Look at the sources on this spread. How do people survive the cold in Antarctica? Write about:
   a) food   b) clothing   c) shelter.
2 Scientists often come to Antarctica for six months at a time. They can spend most of their time living at a research station. Apart from the cold, what other problems might they face?
3 Look at drawing **I**. Suggest why the Halley Research Station has:
   a) generators   b) a food store
   c) a hospital   d) a gym
   e) a radio room.

your expedition...

1 What challenges could you face on your expedition? Think how you would overcome them.
2 What geographical question could you investigate? Suggest how you might investigate it.

F Hypothermia check

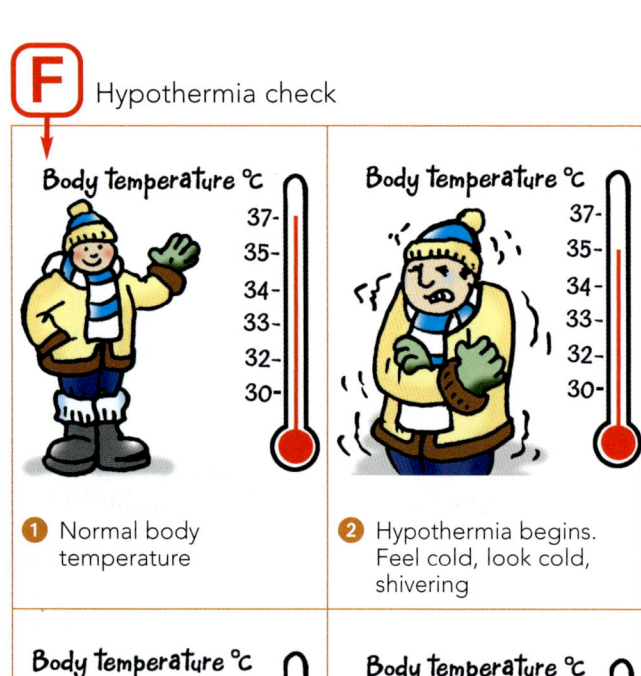

① Normal body temperature
② Hypothermia begins. Feel cold, look cold, shivering
③ Confused, strange behaviour. Some people have been known to take their clothes off!
④ Risk of heart failure. Limbs stiffen up, weak pulse.

The recommended daily calorie requirement for people living in the UK is around 2000 calories for women and 2500 for men. You need to eat more in Antarctica because the body needs more energy to keep itself warm. You are also likely to be more active in Antarctica.

G A recommended diet for someone on an Antarctic expedition

	Energy value (kilocalories)
Biscuits	530
Meat and fish	779
Soup	40
Porridge	22
Muesli	138
Vegetables	120
Butter and cheese	701
Sugar	197
Chocolate	529
Jam	66
Milk	226
Drinking chocolate	46
Dried fruit	201
Rice	84
Pasta	171
Other	164
Total	4,014

Source: British Antarctic Survey

WHY SHOULD WE BE INTERESTED IN ANTARCTICA?

The secret is lots of layers. Layers trap air to provide insulation. Modern fabrics are windproof and waterproof, yet still allow moisture to escape so you don't get sweaty!

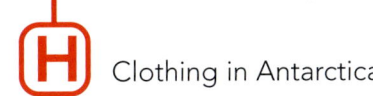 Clothing in Antarctica

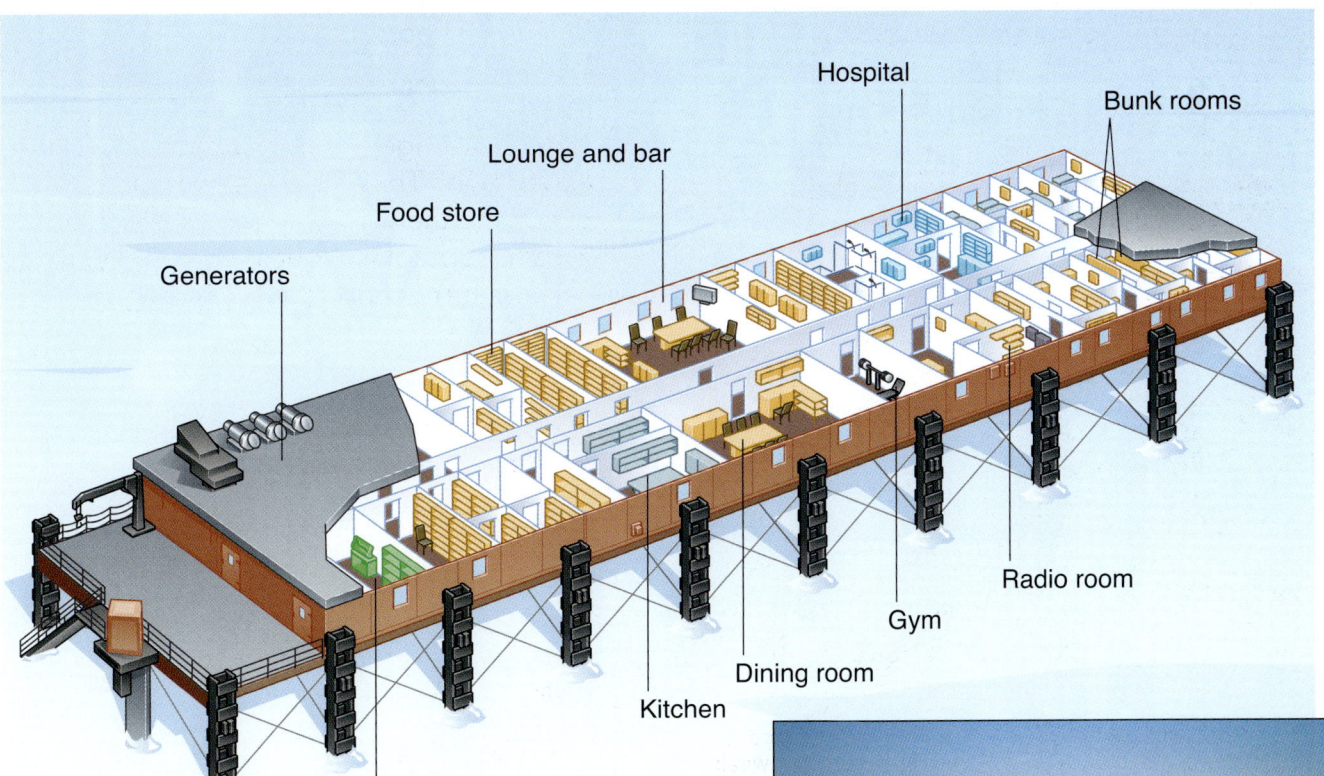

 Inside the British Halley Research Station. Around twenty people spend winter here, and up to 70 in the summer. The building is on steel legs about 5.5 metres above the snow surface. This prevents it from being buried or crushed by snow.

Halley Research Station from the outside

125

ANTARCTICA – THE ULTIMATE CHALLENGE

→ Slowly does it!

Things happen slowly in Antarctica. Nothing rots or rusts in such a cold, dry climate. In 1911, Captain Scott's team built a hut at their base camp before they began their journey to the South Pole (photo **J**). The interior of Scott's hut in Antarctica has hardly changed 100 years later. A bottle of Heinz tomato sauce is still sitting on the shelf and, I guess, it's probably still OK to eat (though no one has actually tried!).

J Inside Scott's hut in Antarctica

Getting rid of waste can be a real problem in Antarctica: either it has to be removed, or it remains there. Modern scientific research stations take waste away from Antarctica by plane or ship to be recycled elsewhere. Dumping of waste at sea, or burning it, is banned in Antarctica.

WHY SHOULD WE BE INTERESTED IN ANTARCTICA?

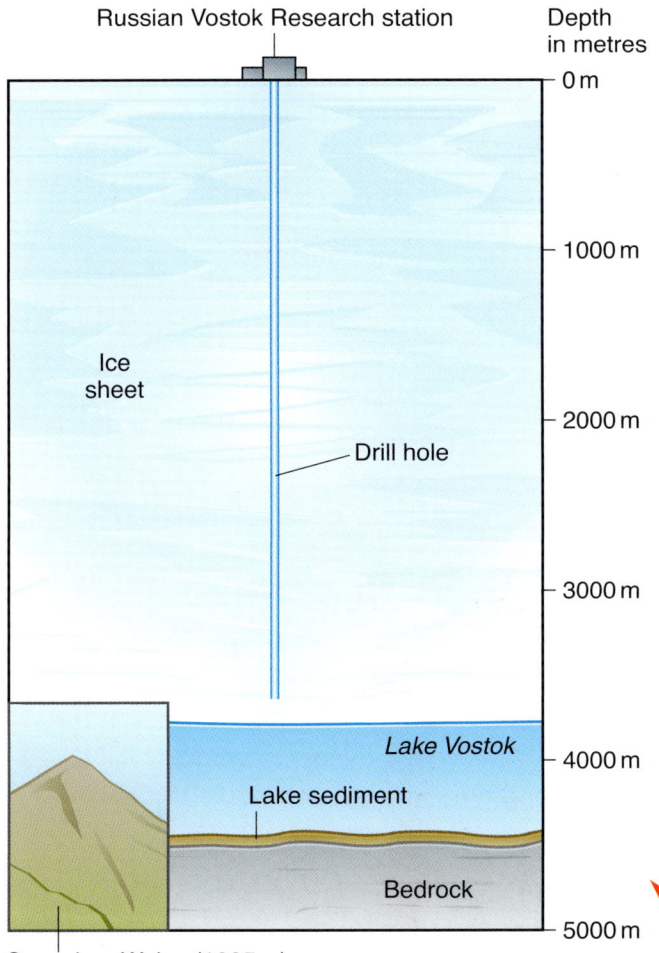

Snowdon, Wales (1085 m) at the same scale

Antarctica is a FRAGILE ENVIRONMENT. On land, few plants or animals survive the extreme conditions. Plants cling to life on patches of bare rock that the ice hasn't covered. Such life is easily damaged by human activity and may take years to recover.

Near the centre of Antarctica, buried 4 km beneath the Russian Vostok Research Station, is Lake Vostok (source **K**). It has been isolated from the rest of the world for half a million years, covered by the ice. No one knows what is in the lake, but it could contain ancient species that have long since disappeared from the rest of the planet, and give us clues about the first life on Earth. Scientists have drilled down through the ice, almost as far as the lake (find out why they were drilling on page 129). However, they have stopped just short of the lake. If they drill into it, they could contaminate the lake and destroy the life that is there. No one knows what to do.

 Should they drill down to Lake Vostok?

activity...

1 Look at photo **J**.
   a) If Scott's hut had been built in Britain 100 years ago, rather than Antarctica, what would have happened to it by now? What would have happened to the tomato sauce?
   b) Explain why this has not happened in Antarctica.
2 a) What is a 'fragile environment'? Write your own meaning (look up 'fragile' in a dictionary if you need to).
   b) Study the information on this spread. In what ways do you think Antarctica is a fragile environment? Give two ways.

discuss...

3 Should scientists go ahead and drill into Lake Vostok, or should it be left alone? You decide.

your expedition...

1 What challenges could you face on your expedition? Think how you would overcome them.
2 What geographical question could you investigate? Suggest how you might investigate it.

ANTARCTICA – THE ULTIMATE CHALLENGE

→ A living laboratory

Antarctica is a great place to do science. The environment is still unspoilt and there is hardly any air pollution that could mess up your results.

Up in the air

In 1985, British scientists (at Halley Research Station) found that the OZONE LAYER was disappearing high in the atmosphere above Antarctica. They called this the OZONE HOLE (photo **L**).

Ozone is the gas that protects us from the harmful effects of the Sun's radiation. Without it we'd get more skin cancer, and other life on the planet would be damaged too. The culprit turned out to be chemicals called CFCs.

L A satellite image of the ozone hole above Antarctica. The hole is the blue area. CFCs are now banned, but they will stay in the atmosphere for years to come. It will take a long time for the ozone hole to disappear.

The ozone layer is a thin layer of gas high in the atmosphere. "Mmm. Lovely sun!"	CFCs (chlorofluorocarbons) were used in aerosol sprays and as coolants in fridges. They can leak into the atmosphere.	Sunlight helps chlorine (Cl) atoms from the CFCs react with ozone (O_3) and turn into oxygen (O_2).
The ozone hole over Antarctica grows to its largest size in spring (October) when the Sun returns to the South Pole. "I can't see a hole!" It is only visible in satellite images!	Scientists discovered the hole by releasing balloons into the atmosphere to measure ozone levels. "It's not even my birthday!"	Over a number of years they found that the ozone levels were getting lower. It was worst over Antarctica. "Bad news!"

WHY SHOULD WE BE INTERESTED IN ANTARCTICA?

activity...

1 Using the ozone hole as an example, explain how our little actions can have unintended effects on the planet.

aim high...

2 Lots of people get confused between the ozone hole and global warming (you studied it in *This is Geography 2*). Study all the information on this spread. Then, explain the difference as simply as you can, as if you were writing for children.

your expedition...

1 What challenges could you face on your expedition? Think how you would overcome them.
2 What geographical question could you investigate? Suggest how you might investigate it.

Deep in the ice

While some scientists are looking up, others are drilling down, and back into the past. By drilling into the ice they are able to collect ice cores (photo **M**). This ice has been laid down over hundreds of thousands of years. By analysing air trapped in the ice scientists can find out how the climate has changed. And, what has happened in the past could help us to understand GLOBAL WARMING.

M Scientists analysing ice cores

Way back, our planet was much warmer than it is today. There was more carbon dioxide (CO_2) in the atmosphere.

"Phew! It's hot!"

Things cooled down during the ice ages because there was less CO_2 in the atmosphere.

"Glad I've got this woolly coat!"

Whatever gases were in the air got trapped when snow fell to the ground in Antarctica. Slowly the snow turned to ice.

A historical record of the amount of CO_2 in the atmosphere is preserved in the layers of ice in the Antarctic.

100 years
1000 years
100,000 years

Scientists drill into the ice to obtain ice cores.

"How far down now?"
"About 200,000 years!"

Chemical analysis of the ice core shows what gases it contains. And that can tell us what the climate was like.

"It must have been cold 10,000 years ago. Not much CO_2!"

ANTARCTICA – THE ULTIMATE CHALLENGE

→ Antarctic meltdown?

The collapse of the Larsen B Ice Shelf

ANTARCTIC ICE SHELF COLLAPSES: GLOBAL WARMING BLAMED
19 March 2002

An enormous floating ice shelf in Antarctica, that has existed since the last Ice Age 12,000 years ago, collapsed this month with staggering speed during one of the warmest summers on record, scientists say.

The piece of ice that broke off was part of the Larsen Ice Shelf, known as Larsen B. The ice was 220 m thick with an area about the size of Cornwall. This was the latest, and largest, of a number of collapses over the past five years. The Larsen Ice Shelf is now only 40% of its original size. The shattered ice formed a plume of thousands of icebergs adrift in the Weddell Sea (see photo below).

Scientists believe the collapse was due to climate warming in the region. Temperatures have risen on the Antarctic Peninsula by 0.5 °C per decade over the past 50 years – five times more than the global average.

Some scientists think that the collapse of the Larsen B Ice Shelf is a warning of things to come. When an ice shelf melts, sea levels don't rise because the ice was already floating in the sea. But, if the Antarctic ice sheet were to melt, that would be a different matter.

Ice shelves form a barrier between the ice sheet and the ocean. They act as a brake, slowing down the rate at which ice moves towards the sea. If the ice shelves around Antarctica melt it would allow more ice to be dumped directly from the land into the sea. Sea levels would start to rise, with huge consequences for us.

However, scientists are not certain that this will happen. Another consequence of global warming could be increased snowfall in Antarctica. That would actually make the Antarctic ice sheet thicker.

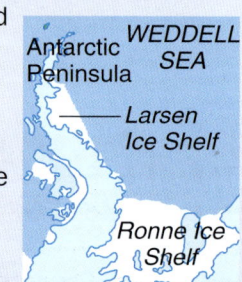

Before — After

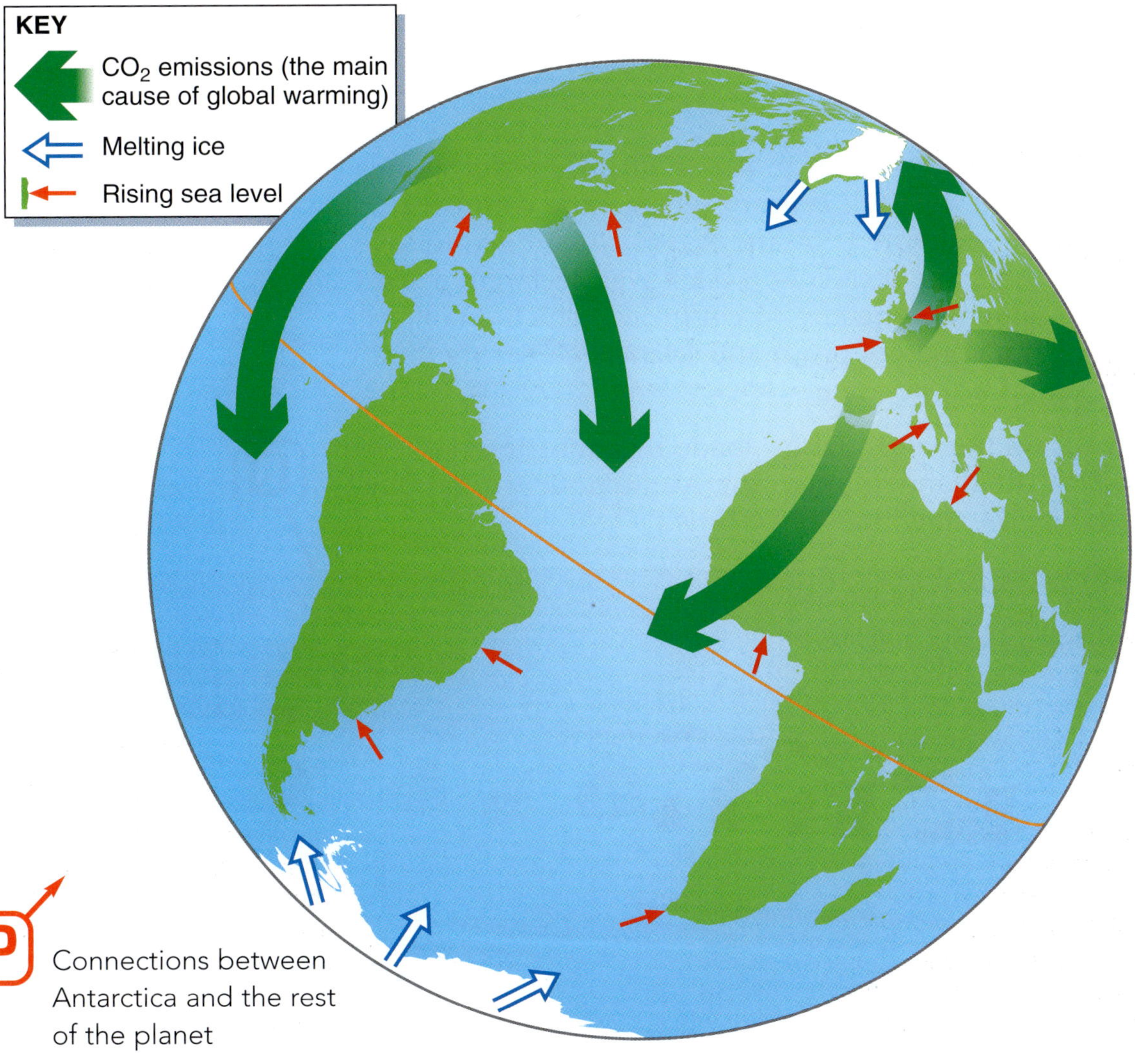

WHY SHOULD WE BE INTERESTED IN ANTARCTICA?

KEY
- ⬅ (green) CO_2 emissions (the main cause of global warming)
- ⬅ (blue) Melting ice
- ⬅ (red) Rising sea level

P Connections between Antarctica and the rest of the planet

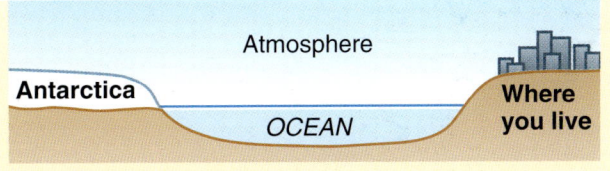

activity...

1 Look at the two photos in **O**.
   a) Identify: **i)** the Larsen Ice Shelf
      ii) the Antarctic Peninsula
      iii) Weddell Sea **iv)** icebergs (broken fragments of the ice shelf).
   b) Draw a sketch of the photo after the collapse of the ice shelf. Label the features.
2 Look at drawing **P**.
   a) Explain how our actions could affect Antarctica.
   b) Explain how what happens in Antarctica could affect us.
   c) Now, draw a large diagram, like the one on the right, to show the connections between us and Antarctica. Label your diagram with your ideas from a) and b).

aim high...

3 Look back at pages 122–123.
   a) What predictions did you make in activity 3?
   b) Does the evidence in source **N** support your predictions? Explain why you were right or wrong.

your expedition...

1 What challenges could you face on your expedition? Think how you would overcome them.
2 What geographical question could you investigate? Suggest how you might investigate it.

131

ANTARCTICA – THE ULTIMATE CHALLENGE

→ Antarctica – the Antarctic Treaty

There has never been a war in Antarctica. However, things became tense in the 20th century when some countries claimed land, while the USA and Russia threatened to take over. As a result, the ANTARCTIC TREATY was declared in 1961. It is an agreement, signed by 45 countries, which establishes Antarctica as a region of peace and science. Under the treaty, all land claims are set aside.

Map **R** shows the land 'claims' made by countries in Antarctica. (Remember, under the Antarctic Treaty no one owns the land – they are only claims.)

 Flags at the South Pole – a sign of peace

The Antarctic Treaty

- prohibits military bases and weapons testing
- requires co-operation between countries to share the results of scientific research
- prohibits nuclear explosions and nuclear waste disposal
- does not recognise any country's claims on territory.

In addition, the Environmental Protocol agreed in 1998 means:
- a ban on mining for 50 years, or until all countries agree to end it
- a ban on killing or interfering with wildlife (e.g. you are no longer allowed to take dogs to Antarctica)
- all waste must be removed (dumping or burning rubbish is banned)
- controls on fishing in the Southern Ocean
- all new activities must be checked for their likely impact on the environment before they are allowed to go ahead.

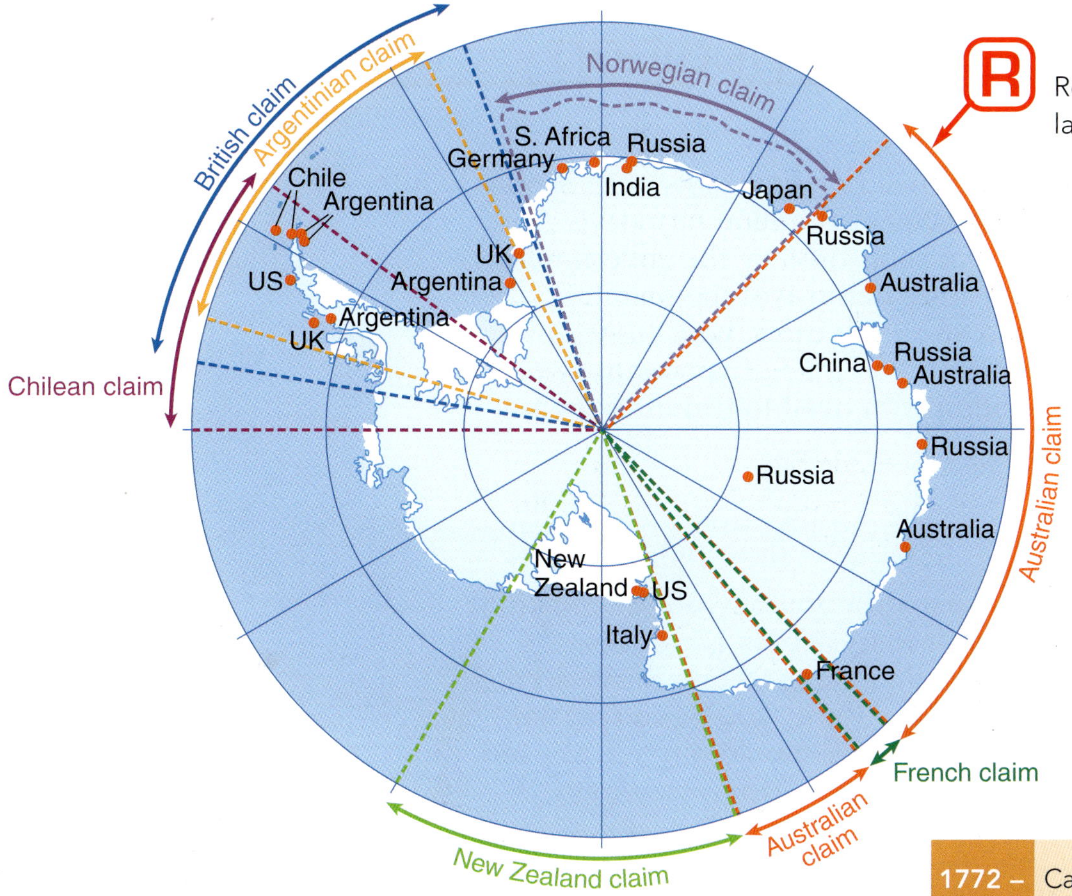

WHY SHOULD WE BE INTERESTED IN ANTARCTICA?

R Research stations and land claims in Antarctica

activity...

1 Look at map **R**.
   a) List the countries with research stations in Antarctica. Which parts of the world are represented here? Are they mainly MEDCs or LEDCs?
   b) Which parts of the world are not represented here? Why do you think this is?
2 a) Name the countries with land claims in Antarctica.
   b) Suggest reasons for each of these claims. The information in source **S** might help.
   c) Do you think any of the claims are justified? Why?

discuss...

3 Work with a partner. Read the statements in the Antarctic Treaty. For each statement:
   a) Why do you think it is included?
   b) Do you think it is a good idea? Why, or why not?

your expedition...

1 What challenges could you face on your expedition? Think how you would overcome them.
2 What geographical question could you investigate? Suggest how you might investigate it.

1772 – 1775	Captain James Cook, the British explorer, leads the first voyage inside the Antarctic Circle
1819 – 1821	Russian expedition circles Antarctica and is the first to see it
1837 – 1840	French expedition is the first to land on Antarctica
1839 – 1843	British expedition (led by Captain James Ross) discovers the Ross Ice Shelf
1898 – 1900	British expedition (led by a Norwegian) is the first to spend winter in Antarctica
14 Dec 1911	Norwegian expedition (led by Roald Amundsen) is the first to reach the South Pole
17 Jan 1912	British expedition (led by Captain Robert Scott) reaches the South Pole.

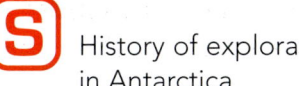

S History of exploration in Antarctica

ANTARCTICA – THE ULTIMATE CHALLENGE

➡ An Antarctic expedition

All expeditions to Antarctica need money – lots of it! Scott's expedition in 1911 cost £40,000 (£4 million in today's money). The expedition was sponsored by the government and by a number of companies because of the scientific investigation that Scott's expedition carried out (not because he went to the South Pole). So, if you want sponsors for your expedition, you need to convince them it will be worthwhile too.

■ your final task...

1 What do you need to take with you on your expedition? Through the unit you have made notes about the challenges you could face on an expedition in Antarctica.
   a) Now, make a list of all the items you need to take with you. The drawings below should get you started.
   b) For each item you take, explain why you would need it.
   c) Finally, just for fun, find out the cost of each item and work out the total cost of your expedition. You could research costs on the internet.

WHY SHOULD WE BE INTERESTED IN ANTARCTICA?

2 What geographical question are you going to investigate?
Through the unit you have been thinking of questions and how you might investigate them.
a) Look at the list of questions you have written and decide which one is the most interesting and important. This is the question that is most likely to win sponsorship for your expedition. The photos are a reminder of some of the important issues you have looked at.
b) Suggest how you might investigate your question. For example, if you decided to investigate the question: 'How do penguins survive here?' you would need to study a colony of penguins in the winter, which is the most difficult time to survive. You would not be able to use tents (you would not survive!) so you would need to stay at a research station.

3 Put your ideas for 1 and 2 together as a proposal to send to possible sponsors. (Make sure that all the items you list in 1 will be essential for your investigation in 2.)

Finally (and again just for fun), think of the sort of sponsors you could send your proposal to. For example, if your expedition is to find out 'How do penguins survive here?', you could send it to an outdoor clothing company that might get new ideas for their clothes from your expedition.

Ice shelf collapse

A fragile environment

Ice cores reveal climate change

The ozone hole

➜ This *is* Geography!

At the start of this course you were asked, 'What is Geography?' I wonder how you would answer this question now you have had three years to think about it?

Here's a reminder of the Geography you have studied in this book…

THIS IS GEOGRAPHY!

activity...

1 Look at the jigsaw pieces on the globe. Find where in the book each photo comes from.
   a) Where was the photo taken? Give the country.
   b) What does the photo show? Write a sentence.

2 At the start of the course, in Pupil's Book 1, you were introduced to seven KEY CONCEPTS, or big ideas, in Geography. These are the concepts that underlie all the Geography you have studied in this book.
   a) Link each concept with a different jigsaw piece. In each case, explain the link. (More than one right answer to this.)
   b) Choose the concept you think is the most important one in Geography. Justify your choice.

discuss...

3 In a group:
   a) Together, decide on the three most important concepts in Geography. If you can't agree, take a vote.
   b) So, what is Geography? Together, produce a definition, no longer than one sentence, to explain what Geography is.

where to next...?

4 Geography can be useful in all sorts of jobs. Think about these jobs:
   - a taxi driver
   - a weather forecaster
   - a city planner
   - a TV or newspaper reporter
   - a travel agent
   - a criminal detective
   - a property developer
   - an international peacemaker.

   For each job:
   a) How could Geography be useful? (Think of some of the big tasks you have done.)
   b) What geographical skills could you use?

5 How could Geography be useful to you in the future? Show your ideas in a spider diagram with you in the centre.

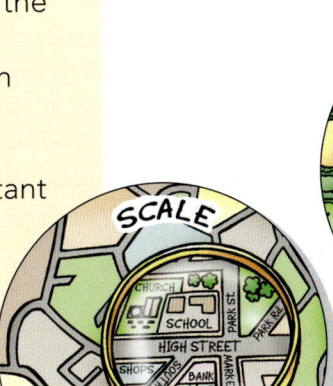

Coverage of Key Concepts

■ Main Key Concept   ■ Other Key Concepts

Book 3	Place	Space	Scale	Interdependence	Environmental interaction and sustainable development	Physical and human processes	Cultural understanding and diversity
1 Living on the edge	Indonesia	Plate boundaries and global distribution of earthquakes + volcanoes	National and global		Impact of tsunami, earthquakes + volcanoes on people	Tectonic processes – earthquakes, volcanic erruptions + tsunamis	
2 Save the rainforest!	Eden Project, Cornwall Amazon rainforest, Brazil	Global distribution of biomes. Rainforest + deforestation in Brazil	Local, regional, global	Our use of rainforest products. Regional + global impact of deforestation	Indigenous people living sustainably in forest. Impact of modern human activities on rainforest	Ecosystem	Learning about sustainable living from other cultures. Attitudes of different groups to rainforest exploitation
3 India – a developing story	India – including Narmada Valley, Kerala + Hyderabad	Population distribution	National – including regional case studies	Historic and present day links between India + UK. Impact of globalisation	Consequences of large-scale development project on environment	Development – including top-down, bottom-up, outside-in (globalisation)	Values and attitudes to development through the eyes of young people in India and the UK
4 Food for the future	Ghana – cocoa production	Global pattern of food consumption	Local, national, global	Food miles LEDC + MEDC food consumption. Trade in cocoa	Organic farming Impact of modern farming on environment	Farming using organic + conventional methods Trade and fair trade	Exploration of values + attitudes to food
5 The Olympics come to town	Olympic Park, Lower Lea Valley, London	Olympic Park and other venues in London	Local, city, national and global	Potential impact of Olympics on Lea Valley	Sustainable development of Lower Lea Valley	Urban regeneration	
6 Israel/Palestine – a land divided	Palestine/Israel	Division of land between Palestine + Israel, changing borders	Local, regional, international	Historic and present day conflict between Israel + Palestine		Migration	Appreciate how and why values + attitudes differ about Middle East
7 Antarctica – the ultimate challenge	Antarctica	Territorial claims in Antarctica	Continental, global	Scientific research and other human activities in Antarctica	Causes + consequences of ozone hole + global warming	Glaciation + ice movement. Ozone depletion. Global warming + ice melting	Values + attitudes to Antarctica's future

Glossary

A

ACTIVE VOLCANO a volcano that has recently erupted or is still erupting

ADAPT to fit in, or change, to meet conditions in the environment

AFTERSHOCK small earthquake that sometimes follows a bigger one

ANTARCTIC TREATY an agreement signed by 45 countries to protect Antarctica as a region of peace and science

AQUIFER a layer of rock that can hold water in its pore spaces

ASH fine particles of rock thrown from a volcano when it erupts

B

BEDROCK solid rock which lies beneath the soil (or ice)

BIODIVERSITY the variety of plants and animals in a place

BIOME a major type of environment or ecosystem, for example tropical rainforest

BORDER the boundary between two countries

BOTTOM-UP DEVELOPMENT development that starts with people in local communities

BUTTRESS ROOTS large roots that grows above ground to support the weight of a tall tree

C

CANOPY the top layer of trees that shades the forest floor from the Sun

CONE the upturned-V shape of a volcano

CONTINENTAL CRUST part of the Earth's crust beneath the land

CORE the middle part of the Earth, below the mantle

CRATER the depression at the top of a volcano from which lava and ash erupt

CREVASSE a vertical crack in the ice

CROP ROTATION changing crops between fields on a farm from year to year

CRUST the thin outer layer of the Earth

D

DAM a barrier built across a river to create a lake

DEFORESTATION cutting down and removal of trees to clear the land

DEPRIVATION poverty

DESALINATION removal of salt from seawater to produce drinking water

DEVELOPMENT improvement in people's quality of life

DEVELOPMENT INDICATOR a way of measuring changes in the level of development

DORMANT VOLCANO a volcano that has not erupted for many years

DROUGHT a prolonged period of dry weather

E

EARTHQUAKE a sudden, violent movement in the Earth's crust

ECOSYSTEM a community of plants and animals in their environment

EMERGENT TREE a tall tree that grows above the canopy of the forest

EPICENTRE the point on the Earth's surface above the origin of an earthquake

EPIPHYTE a plant that grows on a tree for support

EVACUATE to move people from an area of danger

EVAPOTRANSPIRATION loss of water by evaporation from plants and the soil

EVERGREEN keeps leaves throughout the year

EXTINCT VOLCANO a volcano that has not erupted within historic times

F

FACTORY FARMING factory-like farming where animals are kept indoors

FAIR TRADE a form of trade that provides a better deal for farmers in poor countries

FAULT a crack in the Earth's crust

FERTILE good for growing crops

FERTILISER material used to improve the fertility of the soil for farming

FOCUS the point below ground where an earthquake occurs

FOOD MILES/KILOMETRES the distance food travels to reach your plate

FRAGILE ENVIRONMENT a natural environment that could be easily damaged by people

G

GDP/CAPITA GDP divided by population as a measure of a country's average wealth

GLOBAL WARMING the way temperatures around the world are rising

GLOBALISATION the way jobs, people and ideas move around the world

GROSS DOMESTIC PRODUCT (GDP) the total value of all the goods and services produced in a country

GROUNDWATER water that sinks into the ground

H

HUMAN DEVELOPMENT INDEX (HDI) a measure of development used by the United Nations to compare countries

HYDRO-ELECTRIC POWER (HEP) electricity generated by fast-flowing water

HYPOTHERMIA a condition caused by very low body temperature

I

ICE SHEET a large expanse of ice covering a land mass

ICE SHELF a sheet of floating ice on the sea

ICEBERG a floating lump of ice in the sea that has broken off an ice shelf or ice sheet

INEQUALITY lack of equality in wealth

IRRIGATION supply of water to the land for farming

139

GLOSSARY

L
LAVA molten rock from a volcano
LESS ECONOMICALLY DEVELOPED COUNTRY (LEDC) a poorer country with low GDP/capita
LIANA a climbing plant which grows on trees in tropical forests

M
MAGMA molten rock beneath the Earth's surface
MANTLE the middle layer of the Earth between the crust and the core
MID-OCEANIC RIDGE the line where two plates are moving apart beneath the ocean, forming new crust
MIXED FARM a farm growing crops and keeping animals
MONSOON a seasonal wind that brings rain to south-east Asia
MORE ECONOMICALLY DEVELOPED COUNTRY (MEDC) a richer country with high GDP/capita
MUDFLOW a mixture of soil and rain or melting snow that flows down a volcano

N
NATURAL HAZARD a natural event that causes danger for people, for example earthquake

O
OCEANIC CRUST part of the Earth's crust beneath the ocean
ORGANIC FARMING farming without the use of artificial chemicals
OUTSIDE-IN DEVELOPMENT development based on foreign investment
OUTSOURCE to sub-contract, or send work to another company, often abroad
OZONE HOLE a loss of ozone from the ozone layer caused by CFCs (chlorofluorocarbons)
OZONE LAYER the layer of ozone gas found high in the atmosphere

P
PESTICIDE chemical used in farming to kill insect or animal pests
PLATE a large segment of the Earth's crust
PLATE BOUNDARY the line where two plates meet
POPULATION STRUCTURE the make up of a country's population by age group
PROCESSED GOOD a product made by processing a raw material, for example chocolate from cocoa
PYROCLASTIC FLOW a cloud of hot ash and gases moving at high speed down a volcano

Q
QUALITY OF LIFE a measure of people's wellbeing

R
RAW MATERIAL a natural material that has not yet been processed e.g. cocoa
REFUGEE a person who flees their home, or country, to live somewhere safer
REFUGEE CAMP a temporary settlement where refugees live, often in another country
RESEARCH STATION a place where scientists live and use as a base for scientific research
RICHTER SCALE the scale used to measure the strength of earthquakes

S
SEISMIC WAVE a wave of energy from an earthquake, felt as vibration or shaking
SEISMOGRAPH an instrument used to measure the strength of earthquakes
SETTLEMENT a place where people live
SETTLERS people who settle in a new place
SLUM a poor area in a city where people build their own homes
SHIFTING CULTIVATION a type of tropical farming where people clear a new patch of forest every few years
SOUTH POLE the point on the Earth at latitude 90°S
STATE a country with its own government
SUSTAINABLE can be continued without harm because it is not wasteful
SUSTAINABLE DEVELOPMENT development that can meet present and future needs

T
TERRITORY land belonging to a country or group of people
TOP-DOWN DEVELOPMENT development initiated by government
TRADE buying and selling of goods, often between countries
TREMOR a small earthquake, or vibration in the Earth's crust
TRENCH a deep valley in the ocean floor formed where one plate is forced down beneath another
TROPICAL RAINFOREST tall, dense forest found in hot, wet areas near the Equator
TSUNAMI a huge wave caused by an earthquake or volcano on the ocean floor

U
UNEMPLOYMENT lack of employment or paid work
UPSTREAM towards the source of a river

V
VEGETARIAN a diet without meat
VEGETATION plants, including trees
VENT a pipe that carries magma to the surface of a volcano
VOLCANO a mountain formed from the eruption of lava and/or ash

W
WATER TABLE the level below which the ground is wet
WILDERNESS a large natural area untouched by human activities
WORLD MARKET PRICE the price at which a raw material is traded around the world

Index

aftershocks 18
Amazon rainforest 32–6
Antarctica 118–34
   clothing needed 125
   diet 124
   exploration of 133
   global warming 130–1
   Halley Research Station 125
   ice sheet 122–3
   Lake Vostok 127
   Larsen Ice Shelf 130
   science in 124, 128–9
   Scott expedition 119, 126, 134
   seasons 120
   temperature 120
   waste disposal 126
Antarctic Treaty 132–3

biomes 28–9
   Eden Project 40
   see also tropical rainforests
birth rates 49

call centres, India 62–3
chocolate 78–9
cocoa farming 78–83

death rates 49
deforestation 36–9
deprivation indicators 99
development 43, 64
   bottom-up 60
   Human Development Index 55
   outside-in 62–3
   top-down 58–9
   see also India
development indicators 50, 54

Earth
   plate movement 13–14, 15
   structure of 12–13
earthquakes 14–19
   aftershocks 18
   in Britain 24
   in Indonesia 5–6, 7, 11, 14, 18–19
   location of 10
   seismic waves 12, 16
East India Company 56
ecosystems 26, 28–9
Eden Project, Cornwall 40

factory farming 72–3
fair trade 82–3
Fairtrade Foundation 83
farming
   cocoa 78–83
   factory 72–3
   mixed 76
   organic 74, 76–7

   in rainforests 32–5
   shifting cultivation 32–3, 34
food 68–84
   food miles 68–9
   grain consumption 70, 73
   obesity 70
   recommended calorie intake 70
   vegetarianism 73
   see also farming

GDP (gross domestic product) 9, 51
globalisation 62–3
global warming 39, 69, 129, 130–1

Halley Research Station, Antarctica 125
Human Development Index (HDI) 55
hypothermia 124

India
   development in 43–64
   education in Kerala 60
   history of 56–7
   inequality 50–1
   Narmada Valley project 58–9
   and outsourcing 62–3
   population structure 48–9
   Prita's journey to 44–5
   and UK 45, 46–7
International Olympic Committee (IOC) 86
Israel/Palestine conflict 102–15
   history of 104–5
   Netzarim attack attempt 103
   Palestinian refugees 104, 106–7
   security wall 112–15
   water supplies 110–11
   West Bank settlements 104, 108–9, 112

Kerala: education in 60
Krakatau (volcano) 22–3

Lake Vostok, Antarctica 127
Larsen Ice Shelf, Antarctica 130
LEDCs (less economically developed countries) 54, 57, 82
life expectancy 49

MEDCs (more economically developed countries) 54, 82
Merapi (volcano) 20–1
mixed farming 75

Narmada Valley project, India 58–9

natural hazards 4–24

   earthquakes 5–6, 10, 12, 14, 16–19, 24
   tsunamis 4–9, 23
   volcanoes 10–11, 14, 20–3
obesity 70
Olympic Games 86–100
   backing for bid 100
   bidding for 86–7
   candidate cities 86, 88–9
   legacy 86, 98–9
   Olympic Park 86, 90–1, 93, 98
   Olympic venues 86, 92–3
   sustainability 86, 96–7
   transport 86, 94–5
organic farming 74, 76–7
outsourcing 62–3
ozone hole 128

Palestine, see Israel/Palestine conflict
plate boundaries 13–16
population structure: India 48–9
Prita: journey to India 44–5

Richter Scale 16–17

seismic waves 12, 16
shifting cultivation 32–3, 34
Soil Association 74
Survival International 37
sustainability
   Amazon rainforest 32–3
   Olympic Park, London 96–7

tropical rainforests 26–7, 30–9
   Amazon 32–6
   deforestation 36–9
   exploitation of 32–5
   ownership of 34–5
   rainforest products 33
tsunamis 4–9, 23
   early warning systems 9

United Kingdom (UK)
   earthquakes 24
   and India 45, 46–7

vegetarianism 73
volcanoes 14–15, 20–3
   Krakatau 22–3
   location of 10–11
   Merapi 20–1

water supplies
   Narmada Valley project 58–9
   Israeli/Palestinian 110–11
West Bank settlements 104, 108–9, 112

Acknowledgements

The Publishers would like to thank the following for permission to reproduce copyright material:

Acknowledgements
p.30 Nick Middleton, a journey into the tropical rainforest from *Surviving Extremes* (Pan Books, 2004); **p.37** Survival International, information on the Awá tribe from http://survival-international.org.uk; **p.44** Prodeepta Das, from Prita Goes to India (Frances Lincoln Children's Books, 2005), copyright © 2005, reproduced by permission of Francis Lincoln Ltd; **p.71** Erik Millstone and Tim Lang, from *The Atlas of Food: Who Eats What, Where and Why* (Earthscan, 2002); **p.74** Soil Association, logo and text reproduced by permission of the publisher; p.77 RSPB, graph showing bird numbers in the UK since 1970; **p.78** Divine Chocolate Ltd, "What is in a bar of chocolate?" (The Day Chocolate Company); **p.79** The Economist, table of the world's top cocoa producers and consumers from *The Economist Pocket Book of Figures* (2007); **p.81** ICCO, graph of world market price for cocoa 1980-2005; **p.83** FAIRTRADE Mark With permission of the Fairtrade Foundation; **p.86** Olympic logo Reproduced with permission from International Olympics Committee; **p.98** London Borough of Newham, comparative statistics on social deprivation; **p.105** United Nations and World Bank, Israel and Palestinian territories compared; **p.106** Elias Chacour, from Blood Brothers (Chosen Books, 1987), reproduced by permission of Baker Publishing Group; **p.107** Dan Smith, map showing where Palestinian refugees live today from *Atlas of War and Peace* (Earthscan, 2003); **p.109** Zeev Saffer, on Elon Moreh from *Mideast Outpost*; **p.112** Chris McGreal, "The pounds 1m-a-mile wall that divides a town from its own land of plenty" (adapted) from *The Guardian* (26 November 2002), reproduced by permission of Guardian News & Media; **p.114** Christian Socialist Movement, from *Barriers to Peace? - Perspectives on the Barrier* (2004); **p.124** British Antarctic Survey, schools pack on "Antarctica", reproduced by permission of British Antarctic Survey; **p.130** "Antarctic ice shelf collapses: global warming blamed", adapted by John Widdowson (originally published by Associated Press, 19 March 2002).

Photo credits
Cover *l* © Eye Ubiquitous/Alamy, *r* Robert Harding Picture Library; **p.4** © Digital Globe, Eurimage/Science Photo Library; **p.5** © Digital Globe, Eurimage/Science Photo Library; **p.7** © JOHN RUSSELL/AFP/Getty Images; **p.11** © ONNY TUMBELAKA/AFP/Getty Images; **p.12** © JulienGrondin/istockphoto.com; **p.16** © Furchin/istockphoto.com; **p.18** © AFP/AFP/Getty Images; **p.20** © ISMOYO/AFP/Getty Images; **p.23** © Charles O'Rear/CORBIS; **p.24** © Dave Higgens/PA Photos; **p.29–27** © John Harper/Corbis; **p.27** *bl* © Brasil2/istockphoto.com; **p28** *t* © JACQUES JANGOUX/Rex Features, *b* © Lindsay Moller/Newspix/Rex Features; **p.29** *t* © Dennie Cody/Taxi/Getty Images, *b* © Bob Stefko/Riser/Getty Images; **p.32** *t* © Wolfgang Kaehler/CORBIS, *c* © Victor Englebert/Time Life Pictures/Getty Image; **p.34** © AP Photo/Silvia Izquierdo/PA photos; **p.36** © Gregg Newton/Corbis; **p.37** © JUSTIN SUTCLIFFE/Rex Features; **p.38** © Stockbyte/Photolibrary Group Ltd; **p.40** *l* © Kevin Jarratt/iStockphoto.com, *r* © Jason Hawkes/CORBIS; **p.41** *l* © JACQUES JANGOUX/Rex Features, *c* © Gregg Newton/Corbis, *r* © Stockbyte/Photolibrary Group Ltd; **p.42** *tl* © Photodisc/Photolibrary Group Ltd, *tr* © Sucheta Das/Reuters/Corbis, *bl* © Everett Collection/Rex Features, *br* © Frédéric Soltan/Sygma/Corbis; **p.43** *tl* © Dinodia Images/Alamy, *tr* © STR/AFP/Getty Images, *bl* © Sipa Press/Rex Features, *br* © Fotex/Rex Features; **p.44–49** all © Prodeepta Das; **p.50** *t* © Prodeepta Das, *b* © Sipa Press/Rex Features; **p.52–56** all © Prodeepta Das; **p.58** ©T.C. Malhotra/Getty Images; **p.59** © JUPITERIMAGES/Brand X/Alamy; **p.60** © Amanda Koster/Corbis; **p.61** *tl* © Robert Harding World Imagery/Corbis, *tr* © Marco Secchi/Rex Features, *bl* © Amanda Koster/Corbis, *br* © Brooke Slezak/The Image Bank/Getty Images; **p.62** © Jon Hicks/Corbis; **p.63** © Sherwin Crasto/Reuters/Corbis; **p.64** © Prodeepta Das; **p.65** *t* © JUPITERIMAGES/Brand X/Alamy, *c* © Amanda Koster/Corbis, *b* © Jon Hicks/Corbis; **p.66** © Ingram Publishing Limited; **p.67** © Stockbyte/Getty Images; **p.72** © vario images GmbH & Co.KG/Alamy; **p.73** © Julian Simmonds/Rex Features; **p.74** © Organic Picture Lib/Rex Features; **p.75** © Nigel Cattlin/Science Photo Library; **p.76** *tr* © PhotoAlto, *c* © John Widdowson, *bl* © Terry Andrewartha/Nature Picture Library/Rex Features; **p77** © Andrew Fox/Corbis; **p.80** *t* © Kim Naylor/courtesy of Pa Pa Paa, *b* © Pa Pa Paa; **p.81** © Murtin/SoFood/Corbis; **p.82** © Kim Nayler; **p.83** © Divine Chocolate Ltd; **p.84** © Patrick Eden/Alamy; **p.87** © IOC Olympic Museum/Allsport/Getty Images; **p.90** © GetMapping plc supplied by Skyscan.co.uk; **p90–91** © London 2012 via Getty Images; **p.92** © Press/Rex Features; **p.93** © Jonathan Hordle/Rex Features; **p.94** © STUART CLARKE/Rex Features; **p.95** © Berehulak/Getty Images; **p.96** © Scott Barbour/Getty Images; **p.97** both © London 2012; **p.101** *tl* © London 2012 via Getty Images, *tr* © Berehulak/Getty Images, *cl* © Scott Barbour/Getty Images, *cr* © London 2012, *bl* © Press/Rex Features, *br* © London 2012; **p.102** © MENAHEM KAHANA/AFP/Getty Images; **p.104** *t* © Israelimages/Rex Features, *b* © Photodisc/Photolibrary Group Ltd; **p.106** © World Religions Photo Library/Alamy; **p.107** © AWADAWAD/AFP/Getty Images; **p.108** © PEDRO UGARTE/AFP/Getty Images; **p.112** © AP Photo/Brennan/PA Photos; **p.114** © KPA/Zuma/Rex Features; **p116–117** © J.G. Paren/Science Photo Library; **p.119** © J.G. Paren/Science Photo Library; **p.122** © Gerald Kooyman/Corbis; **p.123** © Steve Bloom Images/Alamy; **p.125** © Robert Weight; Ecoscene/CORBIS; **p.126** *c* © Rex Features, *tr* © David Vaughan/Science Photo Library; **p.128** © NASA Goddard Space Flight Centre (NASA-GSFC); **p.129** © George Steinmetz/Corbis; **p.130** *l* © MODIS images from NASA's Terra satellite, National Snow and Ice Data Center, University of Colorado, Boulder, *r* © NASA/Goddard Space Flight Centre Scientific Visualization Studio; **p.132** © Bryan & Cherry Alexander Photography/Alamy; **p.135** *t* © NASA/Goddard Space Flight Centre Scientific Visualization Studio, *c* © Rex Features, *b* © George Steinmetz/Corbis; **p.136** *1* © JOHN RUSSELL/AFP/Getty Images, *2* © Stockbyte/ Photolibrary Group Ltd, *3* © Sipa Press/Rex Features, *4* © vario images GmbH & Co.KG/Alamy, *5* © London 2012 via Getty Images, *6* © MENAHEM KAHANA/AFP/Getty Images, *7* © NASA/Goddard Space Flight Center Scientific Visualization Studio.

t = top, *b* = bottom; *l* = left, *r* = right, *c* = centre

Every effort has been made to contact and acknowledge ownership of copyright. The publishers will be glad to make suitable arrangements with any copyright holders whom it has not been possible to contact.